Dreamland

A Quest for Balance

Kenneth S. Carter

Dedication

Dedicated to the memory of my great-mom.

Acknowledgment

Deep gratitude to those who've ignited my passion for pursuing my dreams.

To my loving parents, thank you for your unwavering support and unconditional love.

To the memories of my beloved grandparents, Granny and Papau, and Great Aunt Joye, your enduring love and legacy continue to inspire me.

And to my cherished family and friends, your encouragement has been the wind beneath my wings. Your presence has made every step worthwhile.

Thank you all from the very depths of my heart.

About the Author

Native Texan Kenneth S. Carter, hailing from Lubbock, developed a passion for art and confectionery at a tender age. Growing up, he assisted at his family's restaurant, fostering his culinary interests.

At just six years old, Kenneth began exploring his creativity through painting and making chocolate at home as a cherished hobby. He honed his chocolatier skills at a renowned chocolate school in San Francisco, where he later furthered his education at Texas Tech University after high school.

Today, Kenneth seamlessly blends his artistic talents with his love for chocolate, creating exquisite and delicious masterpieces.

Contents

Chapter 1: Innocence Amidst Allergies

Not everyone is perfect in this world; every individual has to face some difficulties and obstacles to get through this life, whether they have special abilities, not having enough money, relationship issues, work problems, or even things some of us might have never even thought about. This proves the saying that each one of us is fighting a battle nobody knows about.

However, during such difficult times, all that matters is who you are surrounded by. We all have people who help us get through our challenges. With the help of those people, we enjoy our lives to the fullest. Those people could be our family, friends, or even a stranger. In my story, that person was my mom, and with her, I enjoyed my childhood despite the challenges. I fostered the deepest and strongest connection with my mom while overcoming societal norms and breaking traditional gender roles.

I grew up in a unique and diverse Texas City setting with both industrial elements and a charming touch of flatlands and cottonfields. I lived in the Lubbock area, which produces thirty to forty percent of the world's cotton. My childhood was also unique and full of different hobbies that my mom and I used to do together. As far as the challenges of my life in early childhood are concerned, I was two years old when I was diagnosed with asthma and epilepsy, along with being allergic to grass and cigarette smoke. I could not go outside when the grass was being cut because it would give me headaches and fits of sneezing. For that purpose, my parents came up with a creative solution and replaced the grass in our front yard with rocks. So, we had rocks and pine trees in our front yard. Since my mom could not take me out to amusement parks and other fun places, she initiated some indoor hobbies for me, and we would enjoy those while staying in our house.

I also made my first friend at the age of two, when I used to go to St. Luke's for my preschool. My mom called the teacher for the contact number of one of the kids' mothers, David's mom. The teacher gave her the number of David's mom, Molly. My mom called her and set the playtime. When we went to David's home at the decided playtime, Molly received us with a warm welcome, and my mom greeted her. Then David and I started to play on the floor. Both of our moms were sitting on the sofa watching us play when David's mom, Molly, said, "You know, I don't remember seeing Scott in David's class."

My mom said, "I don't remember seeing David in Scott's class either," and it turned out that the teacher mistakenly gave the wrong number to my mom. However, we had become friends till then, and when our mothers watched us getting along together, they let it be as it was, and David and I stayed friends.

Then, I met my other best friend, Ronnie. His family moved in at the other end of my block. It was in 1975 when one day, my mom and I were outside our home, and we saw

Ronnie coming down toward our house, and then we saw his parents coming after him. So, while my mom met his parents, I got along with Ronnie and became best friends. So, growing up, I had two best friends; one was David, whom I met when I was two, and he was just three months younger than me. Ronnie was a year younger than me. I met him at the age of five when Ronnie was four years old. He would often come down to my house on the weekends because both his parents used to work.

I remember that once, on Christmas Eve, my mom gifted me roller skates. I was a six-year-old then, and I learned skating with my mom in our front yard. My mom learned to skate with me as well because when she was growing up, it was not appropriate for girls to roller skate, ride bicycles, and do all other activities due to some gender-associated activities.

So, when I started learning roller skating with my mom, it was not fun just for me but for her as well. I also have a blurry memory of once when I was making pumpkin pies with my mom, and I cut my hand with the knife. It did not hurt until I looked down at my hand and saw the blood flowing out. The cut was deep, and it needed stitches, but as a child, I was scared of stitches, so my mom called the man from the local neighborhood pharmacy drugstore, which was in our neighborhood, and according to his instructions, my mom wrapped a butterfly bandage around my wound. Therefore, due to that wound, we had to take a break from our activities and rest so that I could get better.

Then, as time passed, I got better, and my mom started teaching me arts, crafts, and painting. I had always been keen to learn to paint with my mom. So, when we began the activity initially, I slowly started to take an interest in painting, and surprisingly, I was a quick learner. One morning, when my mom woke up and came to my room to check up on me, she did not find me on my bed. She walked down toward the two hallways of my home that were connected and shaped like T. She noticed a light on at the end of the other hallway. She came toward and entered the kitchen, where there was a window that overlooked the playroom and the studio where my mom would keep the tools for arts and crafts. She found me there painting. She stayed in the kitchen and kept watching me deeply indulge in painting. I remember that I was painting a picture of a clown at that time, and when my mom saw that, she was so proud of me. Since I was only six years old, I had painted a picture of a clown without the help of any adults.

Talking about different hobbies that my mom and I would do in my childhood, I remember that my mom also started making chocolates with me at home. Sometimes, my friend Ronnie would also join us at our home and make chocolates with us. David would also join us, but not as often as Ronnie.

My mom would color the chocolates and fill them with different flavors. She would give Ronnie and me art brushes, which we used to paint molds like Santa. We would paint his eyes blue and white, and then we would make his nose with a little chunk of dark chocolate in the middle of his eyes. After that, we would paint his eyebrows and hat and then fill it with a solid color of chocolate. From there, we started experimenting with chocolates with different cream flavors and making truffles, too.

Growing up, I started playing and having indoor activities such as arts and crafts, making chocolates, and roller skating with my mom. Then, when I turned seven, I started school. However, I faced obstacles and challenges in my school life because of my asthma and allergies. I could never participate in PE, and I would always sit and watch other children playing. I also got sick for over six weeks and stayed home, and my school teachers gave me projects to do at home that my mom would do. Our teachers also assigned spelling and reading projects to both me and my mother. My mom and I would do those projects at home until I got better and started going to school again.

I remember that was the time when I told my mother that I wanted to start making chocolates and give them to Daddy to sell at the restaurants at the cash register counter with other candies, but for some reason, we could not do it. However, my mom and I still did not stop experimenting with chocolates. Whenever we experimented with chocolate, we put it in a little box, and I would take it to my school through the back door, which used to be the kitchen. I would place it there so all the teachers would taste it. Things were going on like that when I turned twelve. I remember one day at school, my teacher, Ms. Robert, asked me, "What did you do last night?" Well, I should have said we worked on designing potholders or did experiments with chocolates, but I said I was doing homework.

To my answer, she stared at me and said, "Homework? What type of homework did you do?" She was curious and confused, knowing that our school was a no-homework school. I believed she thought my homework was related to chocolate, but I told her I was doing history homework, and then she narrowed her forehead more and asked, "How did you wind up with history homework?" to which I told her that our history teacher gave us some research to do. She assured me that she would take care of it as it was a no-homework school. It was also because I had homework that day, so they missed out on having chocolate, but only I knew that fact.

Chapter 2: Chocolate's Precocious Prodigy

In 1979, my parents bought an old building that used to be a granary. It sat across the parking lot from my parents' restaurant and was known as the old red barn. They wanted to open a barbecue restaurant there. Therefore, after buying the building, my mom and I, along with our carpenter James, who was like my grandfather, analyzed the building and tried to decide what they needed to start on. They wanted to remodel the structure as per the restaurant.

So, as we walked into one of the rooms, I looked up and saw that the room's ceiling was high. Observing that ceiling, I wondered if there could be a candy store, so I looked at my Mom and James and said, "There is no way Daddy needs a ceiling that tall for a dining room. I mean, James can build a floor up there, and I can have a candy store."

It was a great idea, and that is when we started to work on taking our chocolate hobby to a professional level. Later, when we returned from the granary, my mom talked to my dad about building the floor for the candy store in the granary. I must say that my dad was very supportive of our idea, so he pulled James off the remodeling of the restaurant portion. He asked him to start building a kiosk for us so we could open our candy store as soon as it was done. Soon, James began working on remodeling the building. When our kiosk was in process, my best friend Ronnie and I would go there and help the workers by taking the panels off the walls and moving the carpet. We often went there to assist on Sunday afternoons when my parents were walking across the parking lot to the restaurant. They would visit there for a minute or two to check how it was going. One afternoon, on Sunday, when we were busy working in the building, we suddenly heard motorcycles rumbling down the street. So, Ronnie and I left our tools on the floor, came out, and locked the door.

We ran toward my parents' restaurant as fast as we could, and it took us about twenty seconds to get there. We entered the restaurant and looked out through the window. It was a motorcycle gang who came and apparently had a meeting there. Since that building was abandoned for a long time, they would have meetings or other stuff there. There were weeds three to four feet tall and covered with dirt. We saw that they entered the old barn, and there was also a mobile home park on the other side of the building. After some time, they came out and left.

We told my mom everything, and then on Sunday, my mom, James, Ronnie, and I went to the barn. There were two steps going downward, and then there was the trap door. When we opened the door, there was a small room filled with many hubcaps. Ronnie and I decided to volunteer and clean up the mess.

So, we put our gloves on, wore goggles and a hat, and went down there. We were handing the hubcaps and other stuff up because James needed to fill that room with dirt to pour the concrete on top and make it safe. After finishing the work, we kept the hubcaps out and went to our home. The next day, when we visited again, we saw that the hubcaps were gone along with the other stuff. There was nothing there. It seemed like they swept that away with a broom and cleaned up the mess.

At that time, I used to go to a small private school, and after spring break in the 1980s, my mom enrolled us in the chocolate-making school. The chocolate school had one person from each of the four big chocolate companies there to learn more about chocolate. We would go there around 8:30 in the morning until 6:00 in the evening, with around a thirty-minute lunch break. The training was for ten days in San Francisco.

The school was always warm due to the twelve sets of stoves and ovens operating. Everyone had their workstation on which we would make caramel. In that school, we learned to make a lot of chocolate desserts and candies from scratch, such as caramel, nougat, nougatine, marshmallows, and fudges. We also learned to temper chocolate, and this was fun. I was ten years old, the youngest in the school. My mom enrolled herself in the chocolate-making school along with me.

Mr. Richardson, the instructor and trainer in the chocolate school, only accepted twelve students, including my mom and me, along with couples from Ireland, Switzerland, and Ohio. They were people that the big chocolate companies had hired and sent to that chocolate school to train and learn about chocolate. That was part of their training with their company before they started working within the company. I recalled one day when we were making caramel. I was standing by the counter and stirring my caramel along with my mom. Her arm got a little tired, so she stopped stirring for a few seconds when Mr. Richardson walked up behind her and said, "Pattie, you need to continue stirring your caramel; otherwise, it will become grainy. See, how's Scott doing?" Then Mr. Richardson turned to me and said, "Good job, Scott," then he went around to everybody, criticizing them.

When he left, my mom looked at me and said, "Well, thanks, Scott, for making me look bad," then she smiled. In the training school, they had a huge walk-in freezer where you could take some of your chocolate molds. If needed, cool down faster. You could also paint the mold with chocolate and want it to stick in the freezer to freeze it and shape it accordingly. Then, fill it with caramel, cream, etc.

During the training, we stayed a couple of extra days in San Francisco. One day, we were walking down a street, and we saw a gentleman named Stanley Marcus walking toward a store. He was the owner of Neiman Marcus. We recognized him and told him that we liked his store, and then we walked with him a little. He was polite, and we had a little conversation with him. My mom told him about our business. All in all, we learned a lot there and had so much fun. After completing the training, when we were on the plane to return home, my mom asked me, "Well, what do you want to do when you grow up since making chocolate is fun but it is hard work?"

I was very excited at that time, despite being tired. I said, "I want to be a chocolatier, and I want to make our own brand."

Then, when we returned home, we started working on designing our chocolate molds and making our brand. A year passed in those preparations and designs, and by then, James had finished remodeling the building. We opened our store in 1981, in the springtime, when I was ten years old, about to be eleven in May.

My mom and I always wanted to do everything the best we could. We would always want it to be classy and perfect. We were inspired by Neiman's, so we tried hard to do everything well.

Then, when I was eleven years old, I went to the first market with my mom. Despite being a kid, I was always dressed up in a little suit. However, at every store we would enter, the salesman told us that they do not allow kids in their stores. Then, my mom would tell them he was my business partner and that we had our own store. Then we would show them our business card.

In the one store we entered, the salesman was very impressed that I was well-behaved, and my mom assured him I would not break anything or run around his store. Then, we went in, looked around, and placed an order. Slowly, it was becoming normal for me to go to stores and buy things for our candy store. Then, eventually, we approached Godiva to sell their chocolates, but they believed that Lubbock was not big enough for us to sell their chocolates. However, we had our West Texas gold pralines wrapped in a lovely gold box. Therefore, we approached a lady from Dallas Market; she put our products in her showroom and sold them to some other stores. It turned out to be a good idea.

Several stores bought or had our brand in their stores, but they bought a dozen or three dozen boxes at a time. Then, the lady from Dallas Market called us and told us that Neiman Marcus, the representative, visited her showroom and placed an order. However, we would have to be able to complete 2,000 boxes of praline within a month. Then, we would have to be able to fulfill 2,000 as a replenishment within three weeks.

We didn't think we could do that then because we didn't have that many empty boxes on hand, and it would take at least three months to get the empty boxes. So, we decided that even though that would have been a great way to get our brand out there, we decided to decline to take the order.

As my mom always said, if we cannot fulfill an order, then we should be better off or just thank them for choosing us. However, we can let them know when we are ready for the order.

Nevertheless, for the first ten years, we were open and made our own chocolate brand, West Texas Gold. We had our own molds, pralines, and fudge. Day by day, we were getting busier, making chocolate and my parents' restaurant and the candy store. My mom and I were the ones who would make the chocolate. David and Ronnie would help a little bit in the store because they came to work for us before his 16th birthday.

That was how we started our candy store, and we had our supporters along with us. The great supporter was my father. My maternal grandfather encouraged us to start our own chocolate brand throughout our journey. He was very proud.

Ten years later, around 1991, Nancy with Godiva Chocolates called out of the blue and came out to Lubbock to meet with me and my mom. They told us that now Godiva thought Lubbock was big enough for Godiva chocolates.

Chapter 3: Architectural Ambitions for Chocolate

The construction of our candy store was completed in 1981. Since it was an old granary, we had two floors with small rooms, each about 12 feet long and 8 feet wide. In the middle of the granary, we had one room called the silk room, and we kept ribbons and other packaging stuff there.

On top of the silk room, there was a room called Lookout, where a little chair bed and a TV were used to rest or chill after having a long and tiring day in the restaurant and our candy store. I would go there and complete my school projects. However, sometimes it would get really handy to go up there since there was a window in the room that was locked from inside the room and had a railing.

Other than that, if you would walk down two planks of wood, there was a ladder going down to the other roof for escape in case of fire or any emergency. James had also built chocolate cases for the attic store. They would fit exactly how we needed them to be fixed.

Five of the cases were for chocolates, and others were built in the corner. In the middle of our attic, we had stud walls. We would put track on the studs, the Jelly Belly on one side, and gifts on the other. We also had scented candles, but we had to be very careful with them since the chocolates could pick up the scent of the candles. I did not place them too close. Then, when it was remodeled, it turned out like a

European kind of wonderland, as here we were in the middle of West Texas, walking in Erin. It transformed into a store you would most likely see in Europe, such as Belgium. Then, there was a room to the immediate right: a Harry Potter room. The other room to the left was called Corral; there were figurines made of Italian chocolate and other exciting merchandise in that room. Western and wine themes were used, and two chocolate cases from Belgium, France, Switzerland, and Germany, as well as another chocolate case made in the United States, were placed.

There was also sugar-free chocolate, and to the left, there were Christmas trees, along with U.S.-themed sports items. Texas Tech, Dallas Cowboys, and Kansas City Chiefs were the most popular in that area. Then, on the left, a ramp was going down where one would find an old water wheel with puzzles and chocolate bars, an old-fashioned trunk, the metal one that looked like it had traveled worldwide. We got it for my grandmother and her friend.

Then, at the base of the ramp to the left, there were teas and sample bags of coffee. There was a restaurant called the Beer Garden in another room, but we changed the name to the Garden and Collector's Corner. Then, outside, the theme was like a superhero, as in D.C. or Marvel sci-fi, such as Star Wars and Ghostbusters, Transformers, and Star Trek.

At the exit of the garden, going straight, there was all the loose-leaf tea where the tea was made. In 2022, we remodeled it on a new floor and took out some closets. In the room to the right, there were one hundred and sixty different coffee beans worldwide and gourmet foods. Next, there were fifty different Jelly Belly beans and over twenty coffees from Hawaii and all other islands.

Then, there were two bookcases filled with products from Hawaii, and we were the only place on the mainland that carried these products. It had ornaments, soaps, oil, and a selection of other things. Then we had more trees and other displays in this room, as well as a giant chocolate display with many kinds of hot chocolate, including hot chocolate bombs.

We had forty-two Christmas trees up past Christmas throughout the store, and we kept quite a few of them up around the corner. There was a set of stairs that went downstairs called the wine cellar. It was a restaurant, but we kept Disney puzzles and other unique gifts there. There was a fireplace, too. The building's original construction date remains unknown, and it was initially from Matador County.

We had a barbecue restaurant downstairs, below our chocolate store. There was the attic above, and behind the attic, we had a kitchen where we would make chocolates. We would also bake cakes for the restaurant downstairs, and sometimes, when the restaurant staff would get busier, my mom and I would go and help them.

We also had the jackets James brought for me and my parents and one for himself since his wife used to work at the bowling alley. Those jackets were made of satin and had some designs on the back. James also drew sketches of our building that we used on our labels. My mom and I came up with the idea of a logo, an 'Otto Man.' So, when the computers came around, I redrew the sketch of 'Otto Man' on the computer by myself. When we originally opened our store, we showed the head, the neck, and the bow tie of the 'Otto Man.' However, at the barbecue restaurant, we had a full-Ottoman standing on the dessert page, by machine, with the dessert coming out of it, which was the list of dessert headings with an apron.

James also made the sign board for our candy store, which he had to mount on the back of the building facing the hospital so that people could see our board from the hospital and get information about our candy store.

There was an inspector sitting across the parking lot in his car and watching James put the sign up out front, and then, after he tightened the very last bolt, which took six to eight bolts, the inspector came out of his car and asked James to lower the sign board. It made James angry, but my mom calmed him down, and ultimately, he had to lower the board. So, we faced these kinds of small hurdles during the opening of our candy store.

We had two boards, one for the restaurant, which would say Ottos Attic Store, and the other below, which would say Chocolates, Candies, and Gifts. Then, once, my dad jokingly referred to the gift as unique junk, so we changed the gift to 'unique junk' on the board. So, it was chocolates, candies, and unique junk. There were more interesting things, like some music boxes that looked like an old water mill made out of thin copper. We also had honey with gourmet foods.

However, as I mentioned earlier, the hospital was located one block from our restaurant, and we had customers from there. They would tell us that they had seen our sign board from the hospital, and then they came here.

I enjoyed working at my candy store; it was not a chore but something I loved to do. My great aunt would often tell me that I should take a day off every week, but since I loved working there, I would always look forward to more work. I started working when I was a ten-year-old, and we did face challenges or hurdles throughout the journey, but we never gave up. We would always come up with different ideas for displays, etc.

Moreover, my mom and I made the desserts for the restaurant in our kitchen. I remember once we overheard a customer asking the managers which bakery the cakes were bought from. They really liked the desserts, and sometimes, the restaurant manager would come up to us and inquire about the time we would need to make a cake for the customer. Since the customers would place the order for the cake and come to pick up the whole cake at home for birthday or anniversary occasions, we would love the customers' positive feedback, especially when David and I started baking the cakes. I remember we were fifteen or sixteen years old at that time.

As we started our chocolate brand in Lubbock, my mom and I began experimenting with more chocolate recipes. When we started our barbecue restaurant, it was named Otto's Granary Restaurant and Bar. When we were practicing making chocolate with different kinds of chocolate molds to get a trademark on our brand prior to opening our store. We also began to design potholders and wooden ornaments. Furthermore, we would paint the wooden ornaments to match the potholder for Christmas ornaments.

Even though I was only ten, I used to design the potholders with my mom. She and I would color them with pencils and think about more unique ideas. We would make the color bandana with colorful hats and fill them with pencil colors. Sometimes, we would also customize the designs according to our customers' preferences. We had made seven different styles of potholders: a Texas blue ribbon, a boot hat, a dog with a green bandana, a chicken, a hen, a star as a badge, and a blue ribbon. On some designs, we mentioned Texas, while on others, we mentioned Lubbock.

Then, after a little search, we found someone to produce potholders. Then, we started making chocolate from different recipes, and eventually, a company named Texas A& M. developed an edible cotton seed. Therefore, it was a unique idea for us, and we decided to make cotton clusters from it. I remember there were customers who would come into our store and ask about the description card on the chocolate that contained cotton seed and white chocolate.

They would say, "What's in it?"

My mom would say cotton seed and white chocolate, and they would ask again, "Yeah, but are they sunflower seeds or pumpkin seeds?

Then, we would reply, "They are cotton seeds. They are edible."

And again, they would say, "It has to be either peanut, sunflower, or pumpkin.

Then, we would tell them numerous times that Texas A&M. developed an edible cotton seed."

Some of the customers would start asking more about how they made them or whether they were chopped peanuts. Nevertheless, that was always interesting since it also became popular in town. We shaped it like a bowl of cotton, with a white top, painted green leaves at the bottom, and a white chocolate filling. We also had some other chocolates shaped like an oiled derrick that were filled with caramel. Next, we had our West Texas gold pralines and fudge.

We also had an amazing experience with truffles and experimented with making a large truffle. We wanted to see how long it would stay fresh. Therefore, we kept it at home and added a secret ingredient to keep it fresh and moist. By experimenting, our outcome was that it could be kept in a freezer, in a zip-lock bag, and could last longer. I remember that we kept our truffle in the freezer after making it and took it out two years later, and it was still fresh and moist. That was a fantastic experience.

Apart from the truffle, the other chocolates we made were not for extended periods. We would make them in small batches and sell them on a daily basis. In our store, we mostly had our own chocolates that we used to make;

however, we had chocolates from Neuhaus chocolates. Those chocolates were from Belgium. However, after we started buying chocolates from Neuhaus, Godiva approached us and said, "Well, we thought Lubbock was big enough, and we could sell Godiva there."

As said earlier, we had approached them before, and they refused, saying that "Lubbock is not big enough for Godiva chocolates." Also, we had already considered Neuhaus chocolates for our store. I recall that Godiva started in 1923, and Neuhaus started in 1896. They started in Belgium and were still shipping to the United States from Belgium. However, Godiva was made in the United States.

Furthermore, we had other collections of Neuhaus, Galleria, and Joseph Smith truffles. Not to mention that the truffles from Joseph Smith were only available at our store or in the Neiman Marcus Catalog in their Christmas edition. Later on, Joseph Smith sold their store to Hershey's, and then Hershey's closed them after a year.

We didn't stop there; we had Jelly Belly's jelly beans. I remember when I was learning painting in my art class in the fall of 1980, we decided to make jelly bean art. After we got done, my mom took the pictures of the jelly bean art we created and sent them to Jelly Belly. They found it very interesting and decided to commission artists for Jelly Belly Art Works and decorating. Once, on Easter, they got a big Styrofoam egg covered with Easter candies they produced for the display after spring. In that display, the hired artists made portraits of different personalities, such as George

Bush, Ronald Reagan, Nancy Reagan, Martin Luther King, the Buffalo Nickel, Marilyn Monroe, James Dean, and the Statue of Liberty.

I remember that after the first or second year of our opening, our customers wanted the special dinner rolls that we had served in the restaurants. So, my mom, dad, and I went to our restaurant, prepared many dinner rolls the night before Thanksgiving, and sold them. We also baked a bunch of pumpkin pies and sold them. We sold seventy-five to one hundred pumpkin pies. Then, we had our Thanksgiving lunch at our restaurant and cooked turkey. So, it was a good time.

I used to go to the markets with my mom to get supplies for their recipes. I got compliments from everyone for my well-behaved attitude because I was fourteen to fifteen years old, and kids usually would not behave in the markets. We went to the Chicago market and then the Atlanta market, and we also went to the Dallas market. I remember people would recognize us but didn't say anything until we got free from our purchases and got ready to leave. Then, they would come to us and compliment me for my behavior. My dad was also in Chicago to attend a restaurant convention, so after getting done with the Chicago market, we returned to the hotel where we were staying with my dad. A pro tennis player was also staying there. So, my mom and I learned to play tennis. Lastly, on our 35th anniversary, we revamped our logo on the computer using the old one.

Chapter 4: Strategic Expansion into Malls

In 1981, when James was remodeling our granary, we decided to open a kiosk at South Plains Mall, and a year later, our Otto's Attic Store at the granary was ready to be opened. That was an excellent opportunity for expansion, and we also needed a place for our store until the Granary was ready, so we agreed on that.

So, my dad took our carpenter, James, from remodeling the building, and he started building our kiosk in the Mall. The South Plains mall, merchants jokingly called it 'Lubbock's free babysitting service.' Parents would leave their kids at the mall, relying on its secure atmosphere. While many children behaved responsibly, others took advantage of the freedom, attempting to shoplift from vulnerable kiosks and stores.

People would love to drive, drop off their kids in the mall, and then return to pick them up in the evening. We took it as an opportunity despite the struggles of kiosks. So basically, in a kiosk, when we had two people inside and needed to get out of it, we had to open a door inside, raise the top counter up, open the door to the outside, and then, after coming out, close it back. Moreover, catching kids in the mall was tough because they would come in, grab an entire jar of jelly beans, and run away. They were out of sight before we could even get out of the kiosk. However, the kiosk had good visibility, and it was beneficial for us to get our name out there in the mall. I remember that during the holidays, we always had our store open and sold a lot more than usual. At one point, the South Plains Mall had to be remodeled, so the workers came into our kiosk with huge pieces of equipment since they had to put a new tile floor down. They lifted the tiles and lights in the kiosk off the ground at night and constructed the tile floor under it. They moved our chocolate cases, put the tile floor under them, and lowered them back down. Afterward, they put our chocolate cases back in place before opening the mall the next day. They did it so efficiently.

After some time in the South Plains Mall, we got the opportunity to move into the Memphis Mall, which was a little strip shopping mall. However, we had a lease set with a man for five years, but our friend, with his brother, talked to him and got us out of the lease two and a half years early. It was the end of 1983.

The Memphis Place mall had an outside entrance and ten to twelve stores. The mall was covered by a two-and-a-half-block area. However, when we were moving from South Plains Mall to Memphis Place Mall, we faced some challenges, as the place we were supposed to move into was not ready because they were painting it. So, they gave us the key to one of those empty stores in the shopping center across the street. We used it for a couple of days to store our stuff. We waited for them to finish the paint and the carpet, then moved to the store in Memphis Mall. They would usually decorate the mall by themselves, but after some years of our moving in, we volunteered to help with the decorations of the mall. So, every year for the next seventeen to eighteen years (since we were in Memphis Place Mall for twenty years), we decorated the entire mall for Christmas. We went from just one Christmas tree, which was about fourteen feet tall, in the middle of the planter on the floor to more Christmas trees in the hall. Someone else did the lights outside the mall; it looked gorgeous. Decorating the mall for Christmas was always fun and exciting.

My mom and I would always enjoy it, along with our workers. Not only did we put trees up, but we also put up garlands and hung snowflakes throughout the mall. Furthermore, for about eight years, we took an area of the mall, put sheets on the floor covered with snow, and added several trees. Additionally, a night-foot-tall gingerbread house with little gingerbread people in front of the house. This display for Christmas was inside the mall; it had a little white picket fence around it. It took up about 12 feet by 10 feet.

We had a store across from the children's store. My mom would go there and buy clothes for me when I was younger. That store was owned by a lady who retired two years after we moved into Memphis Place Mall. She closed her store, so we moved across the hall and got more space. As we had already talked to the mall manager, if the lady ever closed her store, we would like to have that space, so that portion came under our candy store. So, the specialty of that area we acquired was that it was at the corner and had display windows facing outside. Across the hall, there was a Hallmark store and Harrigan's Restaurant. So, in that lady's store, which was called Little Mister, we got after her retirement, and we made our office, which was raised up to eighteen inches. It was in the middle of the store and had three sides; on the fourth side, there was a small jewelry store that we also took over after their closing. We enlarged our office space a bit, and we also had windows in the office, so if we were working there, we could look at the store. I have always been one to be more in-store and hands-on. There were times we had our work done on the computer, but I would rather be out in the store than back in the office.

There was another store next to ours called 'Played Against Sports.' Eventually, they moved out of Memphis Mall, and we expanded our store to their spot, too. That was good for us because we needed space. In this way, our store expanded from about 3500 to 7000 sq ft.

Through expanding and availing opportunities, we got a lot of exposure. The Texas Tech Palm Squad contacted us to visit our store, and we allowed it. So, they came and took pictures in their uniforms in our store for December for their calendar. Moreover, Jelly Belly had sent us their Jelly Belly man costume, so one of our workers got dressed in that Jelly Belly man's costume to greet customers for a week because we had that costume for a few days.

Fortunately, we were on the waiting list with Jelly Belly for two or more years to get some Jelly Belly art to display. So, when we got our turn, they sent their jelly bean art out.

At different times, we had various arts. First, we had the Statue of Liberty Jelly Bean, which was six feet tall and four feet wide. After that, we had the Buffalo Nickel, then James Dean, and then George H.W. Bush for his presidential ceremony. We kept it on display for a few weeks. Then, we had one of Ronald Reagan when he was a cowboy with a hat. It was a Western theme where he was wearing a denim shirt. Sometimes, we would have a contest where customers had to guess the number of jelly beans in the statue.

Along with that, in Memphis Place Mall, our store was right across the hall from Harrigan's, a trendy restaurant, and many people would come there to celebrate their special occasions such as engagements, promotions, anniversaries, birthdays, etc. It was a go-to restaurant in Lubbock for a while, so the customer usually had to wait for their turn. So, they would come and peek their heads inside the door. They would ask us about our closing times, pointing to our candies across the store. So, for their convenience, we would bring the item they pointed out to the door so they could see it. They would not have entered our store since they were in their waiting line, and they could have missed their name being called out by the restaurant.

To solve that issue, we came up with an idea. We bought speakers, connected them with the mall's speakers, and put them in our store. In that way, whenever Harrigan's called out their customers' names to come, they could hear it in our store as well. That idea was liked by the territorial manager of Harrigan's as well.

It helped the customers immensely, as they did not have to wait outside in the mall. They could visit our store, look around, and shop for their favorite candies. That became a really good thing for us and for them as well.

Moving forward, one Sunday afternoon in the Memphis Place Mall, a man came into our candy store and looked around. We had a nice fifteen to twenty-minute conversation as well. I knew he was Gene Simmons from the music group KISS, and he had dinner across the hall. ''

After that, we had Texas Tech's seventy-fifth anniversary, and a lot of people attended. One of those people was a man who looked familiar to me, but I didn't place him automatically off the top of my head. He was looking around the candies, chocolates, and other items in our store, and there was another man who was doing weird things. For example, I saw him coming into my store, and then he went out and exited the mall. Then, a few moments later, he entered the mall again, started to come into my store, and then went out immediately. I was wondering what he was doing.

He repeated this action two to three times, and then he was gone. It was a hectic night, so I got back to my work. A few days later, a lady came into my store, supposed to be the wife of that man who was doing weird things. She told me that he was her husband, and he was a fan of John Denver, who was in my store. So, the man looking familiar to me was John Denver, and the man doing weird things was gaining the courage to talk to John Denver, but unfortunately, he could not. After some time, Harrigan's moved out of the Memphis Place Mall for a year, and that was when I wanted to see who our potential customers were. Who would come into our store for us, compared to the ones who would visit our store just to kill time?

While Harrigan's was gone out of the mall, we remained just as good as we were at the time of Harrigan's, and it was surprisingly good. Moreover, it turned out that some people would come to the mall for us but could not find the parking. One man said he came to the mall for our candy store five times last year, but he could not find the parking place, so he had to go somewhere else. He further mentioned that, now that Harrigan's was out, there was extra parking space in the parking lot, and he could come in and shop.

Therefore, having Harrigan's across the hall was perfect because we entertained their waitlist, which was in favor of their customers and also beneficial for us. However, when it came to holidays, our customers could not find parking outside.

Moving further, we also did commercials for different holidays. The advertising teams would come to our store and film their commercials, and eventually, we got in charge of the Christmas commercial for the mall. Our part was to coordinate with the man who was making the commercial for himself. One time, one of the TV stations was doing a trade, and they needed thirty gift baskets. Then they came to us and asked if they could increase them, and we were cool with that as well.

After that, the same man came back and increased the baskets to ninety for their sales representatives. My mom and I started preparing the baskets, and a couple of days later, the man increased the order to two hundred and ten gift baskets for their clients, and they needed it in two days.

It was fun for us; my mom and I got everything together and started organizing. Between the preparations, we went to McDonald's for breakfast, then returned and started preparing the rest of the order; all in all, we worked forty-two hours straight with a break to go eat or have pizza delivered. We finished them by 8:00 on Friday morning when they needed the order. Then we opened our store at 9:00 a.m. the same day. With all this, we stepped into the year 2004. The Harrigan's came back to Memphis Place Mall after moving out in 2003. While in Memphis Mall, along with the good times, we had some bad times, too. My dad had a quadruple bypass, so my mom had to be in the hospital with my dad, and I had to manage the store alone. It was the week of Christmas in 1996, so James met me and my mom at the hospital. We had Christmas dinner in the cafeteria at the hospital that year, and the food was good. They served turkey and dressing with cranberry sauce.

Then, after some time, we decided in October 2004 that we would move out of Memphis Place Mall in October 2005 since we had the granary in the other building, where we also had the restaurant downstairs and the candy store upstairs. So, we moved back to our granary, which turned out to be exciting. However, we would miss the holiday happenings in 1986. Other than that, we had a booth there every year through 2019. When we were in Memphis Place Mall back in 1969, my parents opened El Chico across the parking lot in September 1969. They bought the building to make Otto's Granary the restaurant and candy store in 1979, and then we were going to put the store upstairs. After about ten years, Corporate came to town and asked my parents if they wanted to put a second El Chico in. My parents said no since they were happy with one.

They insisted and said that if we weren't building another El Chico, they would build and initiate a competition with us. So, we opened the second El Chico location on Slide Road on June 15, 1979, across from the mall. Then, we opened a restaurant named Otto's Granary in 1984; prior to that, we opened the Kiosk in South Plains Mall in 1981.

However, the matter was that the lease was time to renew, and my dad was also sick and in the hospital, so that was a tough time we were going through, and we had to close our second El Chico. Since the shopping center wanted to bring new business in, we moved everything out of there and closed that location. All those employees got jobs at either Otto's restaurant or at the other El Chico.

I remember my manager and me being at my cousin's wedding in Tahoka when we found out about the closing of the restaurant on Slide two days prior. That was the challenge of informing our employees about the closure. Moreover, the storage issue at our candy store was also happening at the same time. We had limited storage, so whenever we got out of stock. We put all the jelly beans in the containers with lids and stacked them in the boxes on each other. Then, there was a place where we would go with all the restocking, park our car by the dumpster, and walk up to the long hallway. We would drop off the chocolate and jelly belly restock orders.

Chapter 5: Culinary Mastermind in the Chocolate Business

Going back to the time when Ronnie, David, and I were teenagers, we would do work for our candy store. David, Ronnie, and I gained valuable experience and skills from helping behind the bar, serving, cooking, washing dishes, working the cash register, and even managing the candy store. We learned every aspect of the business, from top to bottom.

My mom hired David and Ronnie based on their merits. I remember David coming to my mom with his job application, and he was very nervous. My mom said she did not hire him because he was my friend but because of his merit and abilities.

For our pay, we got paid just like everyone else; however, when we were younger, like ten to fourteen years old, my mom had set up an effective system. She divided our pay into quarters and would pay according to the quarters in which we had worked.

We would do small and easy tasks such as labeling boxes and bags, packing pralines, and packing West Texas gold boxes. To be specific, if someone else did our job, he would get five dollars an hour, but since my mom had set the system for us, we would keep track of our quarters by honestly writing them down on our chalkboard. When our quarters would sum up to seven to eight hundred quarters, my mom would go to the toy store and buy us a new Star Wars toy or video game, and then she handed over the receipt for every item to us. We would count and calculate the remaining amount to save and add up in the next pay.

I remember that I would always like to save my quarters, and I did up to fourteen to sixteen thousand quarters. When I received my pay for those quarters, it was enough that I bought my first waterbed, my first stereo unit, my first Apple computer, and my first Apple laser printer to go with my Apple computer. Even after buying these items, I was able to save some money. It was a very effective system; later, my best friend David used it for his daughter.

So, we would open our store from 9:00 a.m. until 10:00 p.m., from Mondays to Saturdays. At first, we would go off on Sundays, but then customers from the restaurant downstairs would want to come upstairs, so we started opening on Sundays from 10:00 a.m. to 6:00 p.m. Eventually, Sundays got busier as well, and it turned into regular weekdays.

Then, we extended our Sunday hours until nine at night. Even when we shifted to Memphis Mall, we would stay open until 11:00 p.m. on Sundays. During COVID, we changed our timings to 10:00 a.m.–6:00 p.m., and Sundays were closed. Then, post-COVID, we changed our timings to 10:00 a.m.–7:00 p.m. I would come early on Sunday mornings, and even on weekdays, I never minded staying late in the candy store. I would only return home early when I had some projects to do or if there were some important works related to my puppies. As mentioned previously, we knew how to make chocolates, which I had learned from my mom, and my best friends learned from me. So, we would also make different sweets from chocolate, and then eventually, we started baking cakes in our attic for my dad's restaurant downstairs.

In our candy store, we would offer free deliveries as well. If someone wanted to order from their office or home, we would prepare the order, and David and I would deliver it. Since I did not have the license at that age, but David did, we both went together to deliver the orders. Talking about deliveries, once we came across a bad situation due to a misunderstanding with our helper, Bobby. She was a lady who used to help my mom in our house and the store. She would also pick me up from school and take me to art classes.

So, one day, a doctor visited our store with his wife, and they bought approximately 35 boxes of chocolate. His wife inquired about the deliveries, and Bobby said, "Yeah, we deliver," and Bobby further asked the doctor's wife, "Where would you like them to be delivered?" to which the doctor's wife said she would get back to us. She did not take those 35 chocolate boxes; instead, she wanted them delivered.

After some days, the doctor's wife dropped the list of addresses, and when Bobby checked the list, multiple addresses were mentioned. Some were offices, and some were homes. It was a major mishap, as Bobby thought the doctor's wife would give only one address for delivery. We counted them, and there were thirty-five different addresses; five or six of them were to be shipped; one was Ransom Canyon, about thirty minutes away from Lubbock. The remaining addresses were in Lubbock.

Fortunately, that case fell on me and David, and it was Christmas time. However, we solved the case very efficiently. First, we organized the addresses by separating the offices and homes. Then we checked the closing and opening times of offices, since those needed to be delivered first. We made a separate list of homes and then started to deliver the order. It was a bit tough to get it done within the time frame, but we did it professionally; we even dressed very neatly and wore a tie, which looked very nice on us.

This did not stop there; the doctor's wife would come every year for ten years at Christmas, place the order for deliveries, and David and I would deliver them. David was in college and would work, so during the Christmas break, we would wind up our store and make those deliveries. Sometimes, we encountered snowfall, so it was a fun and exciting errand.

Apart from deliveries, my friends and I also got hands-on experience serving. Sometimes, the restaurant downstairs would need help, and we would help them serve and set tables for customers. David liked to help in the kitchen, so he worked there, and Ronnie and I assisted in the dining hall. We were only seventeen then and became proficient in serving, setting the tables, cooking, and even dishwashing.

On Saturday morning, David would come early to help in the restaurant by serving breakfast. After that, he would go upstairs to the store and work there. I must say that through all those experiences, we learned a lot, and by the age of eighteen, we were able to help bartend at the front desk.

Moving forward, in the spring of 1988, before my high school graduation, proms were happening at different schools. It was another exciting opportunity, so my mom and I decided to do something special for prom. We set a menu including fish, steak, and a salad with a free dessert. To promote our deal, we designed flyers and distributed them in some schools. The night before the prom was way busier; we worked all night to prepare everything beforehand. So, on the weekend, the prom night went well.

However, the next morning, when I went to school, my teacher told me that an incident had happened at night. Unfortunately, the wrong crowd from one of those schools had gotten our flyers, and they broke into our store at night and created chaos. She assured me that no one was hurt and allowed me to take leave for a week to fix things.

The same day, Bobby came to pick me up early from school. On our way to the store, she told me that when my mom opened the back door of the store, the water flowed out to her feet. She was with the cooks of our restaurant downstairs, and when they came inside, the floor was covered with water. They broke in from the windows, set five small fires, and broke the top of the chocolate cases. It was heartbreaking to see our candy store destroyed. Breaking the cases caused the sprinkler to activate; due to that, the alarm wires melted, and it stopped working. My mom called the firefighters immediately, and I had reached the store by then. I saw the firefighters turn off the sprinklers, which created a huge mess. The policeman had arrived, too; he was a tall, large man who was not letting in the press, media, or other people who did not belong to our candy store.

The firefighters spent approximately twenty-five minutes shutting off the sprinklers and draining the water from our wine cellars, where we stored our wine collection. They brought in three large hoses from various fire stations to manage the task. The water damage was extensive, causing the tiles upstairs to lift and water to leak from several areas, necessitating repairs. This incident was a significant setback, resulting in considerable losses for us.

Despite this, we managed to adapt by temporarily relocating our candy store to the dining room downstairs, allowing us to continue operations. The fireman's pump struggled to drain the water from the wine cellar, a painstaking process that took over four hours to complete. Initially, the first pump malfunctioned, followed by a second one failing to work. They finally made progress when they brought in a third pump from another fire station. Curiously, once the third pump was operational, the other two pumps also began to work, finally helping to clear the water from the wine cellar. After that, in the summer, my mom and I went to New York to visit a fancy food show. When we reached the hotel we had booked, it was under maintenance, and they were changing the air conditioning in all the rooms. Therefore, the lobby of that hotel was jam-packed with people, so my mom decided to book a room in another hotel, and it took her twenty minutes to do so. Then, we attended the fancy food show, which was worth visiting. After that, while in New York, we went to see Arsenic and Old Lace on Broadway and had a good time there.

Our hotel's prime location allowed for leisurely walks through the neighborhood, where we discovered an array of captivating stores. One standout was a chocolatier showcasing a breathtaking, life-sized chocolate Statue of Liberty. This edible masterpiece, protected by plexiglass and cooling vents, was a marvel. As we continued our stroll, we took in the iconic skyline featuring the majestic Empire State Building and the Twin Towers amidst a tapestry of other notable buildings.

Chapter 6: The Tea Leaf Mystery

On Monday, my mother visited her mother's house with my uncle (my mom's brother). During lunch with the family, Uncle asked my mom, "What's your secret to keeping your plants so lively? I'm an avid gardener and want a beautiful green lawn in front of my house."

While they were chatting, Granny showed them her flowers. Uncle noticed that his own flowers were small, about the size of a hand, whereas his sister Patty's flowers were much larger, about the size of a plate or platter. He was curious about the difference.

Patty jokingly, yet seriously, replied, "Well, everything's bigger and better in Texas!" She was hinting that the Texas climate and soil might be contributing to the impressive size of her sister's flowers.

My mom then revealed her secret to her brother Dan. She used tea leaves from the restaurant where she worked as fertilizer for her plants. She would collect the used tea bags in a bucket and take them home to open and spread on her plants. Occasionally, she'd also use coffee grounds. Uncle Dan joked that she should send some of her 'secret ingredient' to him in Oklahoma, but my mom knew he was half-serious.

A few weeks later, back in Texas, my mom and I decided to play along. We filled a Styrofoam box with a trash bag, added the tea leaves, sealed it tightly, and shipped it to Uncle in Oklahoma via bus. It was a lighthearted way to respond to Uncle's request, and we were curious to see how he'd react to receiving a box of tea leaves in the mail.

We were curious about the status of the package we sent to Uncle in Oklahoma. We wondered why it was taking so long for it to arrive and why Uncle hadn't mentioned it. Meanwhile, at our store, Otto's Granary, we received an unusual phone call. The caller asked if we had shipped a box from Texas to Oklahoma via bus, and when I confirmed, the caller thanked us and abruptly hung up. There was no caller ID, so they couldn't identify the caller.

The story takes an interesting turn here. Apparently, someone at the bus station had raised an eyebrow about the package's contents. Since we had reused a box that originally came from GODIVA Chocolates in New York, this was a few months after 9/11, and it's likely that the bus station staff were on high alert for suspicious packages. The reused box had raised some red flags, leading to the mysterious phone call.

The bus station staff grew suspicious when they noticed the box had been to multiple locations, so they contacted the police. The authorities brought in dogs to inspect the package, and the canines detected something unusual, prompting further investigation. The bus station staff was instructed to keep quiet and not alert Uncle or anyone else about the situation. Weeks passed, and the tests continued. One day, a secretary from Oklahoma or Arkansas walked by the detective's desk and asked, "What's the plan with this box?"

The detective replied, "We're still running tests, and Washington is trying to figure out what kind of new drug this is."

The secretary asked to take a look, and the detective agreed, warning her that she wouldn't be able to determine anything.

To their surprise, the secretary immediately recognized the contents and said, "This is tea."

The detective was confused, asking, "What kind of drug is that?"

The secretary clarified, "No, it's just tea – like the kind you use to make iced tea or hot tea." The detective still didn't understand, so the secretary explained it again.

The detective made a phone call to the agent in Washington, who rechecked their findings and instructed them to conduct another experiment.

However, after the additional test, they called back and said, "Dispose of the box and never mention this again."

The police took the box to their lab, but they couldn't determine its contents. The case was then escalated to the Feds, who sent a specialist from Washington to Oklahoma (or possibly Arkansas, given Uncle's proximity to the state border). The Feds agent took a sample of the substance back to Washington for further analysis. For three weeks, the Feds ran extensive tests, trying to extract what they thought were drugs from the tea leaves. However, they couldn't crack the code. The astonishing truth was that the mysterious substance was, in fact, just tea leaves – a harmless and unexpected twist.

The police returned the box to the bus station, where an officer waited to hand it over to Uncle at 4 o'clock. When Uncle arrived, someone shared the incredible story of what had transpired. He was shocked and immediately told Granny to call my Mom and warn her never to send him tea again.

Uncle was relieved that the authorities hadn't searched his motorcycle shop, tearing out walls or inspecting motorcycles for hidden contraband. The ordeal was sparked by the moldy scent of the tea, which had been stored in a styrofoam-lined box and bag. The unique aroma had triggered the dog's alert, leading to the mistaken assumption that it was a new, exotic drug.

Ironically, a James Bond movie had recently featured a plot involving cocaine hidden in fuel trucks. It seemed that the film had inspired someone or was trying to stay ahead of potential smuggling methods. The authorities had gone to great lengths to experiment and separate the supposed drug, only to discover it was just plain black tea – the kind commonly served in restaurants.

Chapter 7: Harmony in Artistry and Education

In the summer of 1980, my mother enrolled herself, my best friend, and me in art classes. In those art classes, we learned to paint and completed two paintings each. We had great fun doing those paintings, which gave my mom an idea for me.

Since I was asthmatic and could not participate in PE, my mom talked to the art teacher, Ms. Mary, about private art lessons. Mary told her she had been giving private art lessons at her house. So, my mom had a conversation with the principal of my school, Mrs. Arwine, about taking art classes in the afternoon instead of going to PE, and she agreed. Thus, I started taking private art classes at Ms. Mary's home from 1:00 p.m. to 2:30 p.m. five days a week. I took art classes from ten until my high school graduation. Even in college, I kept up with the art classes, which helped improve my art skills and painting on canvas. I also learned to paint on glass.

I remember painting on the saw blades that James took off while working on remodeling our restaurant. Those painted saw blades turned into incredible art pieces. Furthermore, some big wheels were rolled up with cable, used by the electric companies while installing new cables. Those were about eight to six feet in diameter. So, James would talk to the workers of electric companies about having those wheels once they had emptied one of them. The workers allowed him to take an empty wheel, and James brought it to Mary's house. On that wheel, I painted and hung it on the wall of Otto's, the restaurant downstairs in the wine cellar. Another painting hung in the room that we named The Beer Garden.

Along with that, I learned to paint on gold leaf with different techniques and on different textures. I would also use chocolate to paint on chocolate molds and Santa Claus with our set of art brushes. I would use them and meticulously paint the eyes of Santa, the hat, and his cheeks. There was a clown made from chocolate, which I painted in different colors. That way, I would utilize my art skills, some in chocolate and some in Jelly Belly art. I also painted and covered with Jelly Beans to make the Ottos-Man for our candy store and the EL-Chico Man for the restaurant downstairs. My mom clicked pictures of them and sent them to Jelly Belly, and within one or two years, Jelly liked our idea to do artwork out of jelly beans. Then, they started commissioning artists from all over the United States to have different art pieces, which became interesting.

I also turned some of my paintings into greeting cards to sell and placed them on our front desk. Luckily, they were liked by the customers. With these experiments, I realized that anything could be done with the skills we learn, as I learned about paintings and did experiments on different things. We gained a lot of profit and customer attention in the market. I had been in these experiments from a very young age, and luckily, I went to a small private school that would not give homework to students. Therefore, I spent the rest of my time with my mom, experimenting with chocolate and painting. However, in college, I had homework, so I learned to balance my work and studies.

I remember, a year after enrolling in art classes, we took sailboat lessons as well, in which we learned to sail a sailboat in a park with a good-sized lake. It was fun and exciting to take a break from artistic skills.

Then, in 1986, they did a remodel at my parents' restaurant, El Chico, the Tex-Mex restaurant. So, Mary and I put our input into remodeling by painting different words over our doorways, like Gracias, Ben Benito, and La Cosine. It took several nights since we used different paint colors and had to let it dry before painting another layer. We did not want the colors to blend. We also painted the wall inside the restaurant across the parking lot from the Otto's. We made four to five huge palm trees on it, ten feet tall and twenty-two feet wide. The palm trees' top branches and leaves went above the windows, so we had to angle the trunks a certain way to shape the palm tree leaves properly. It looked realistic and covered the whole space of the wall. We finished it in a few weeks.

James cut out the El Chico man logo from wood, and then Mary and I painted it. Our design featured the iconic figure against a vibrant sunset backdrop. The sign had a distinctive arch at the top and the words 'El Chico since 1923' written below the logo. It took us several weeks to complete the painting. The finished sign measured approximately 7 feet tall and 10 feet wide. We also painted Christmas balls for decoration in our store and restaurant. With this, I learned to paint on different surfaces or textures, which I greatly enjoyed. I started painting when I was six and took lessons until I was twenty-four. While painting, I would always be careful since I wanted to keep my clothes clean. Sometimes, when wearing a tie, I would tuck my tie into my shirt and start painting carefully. There were times when my mom and I would make our padded hearts and oval boxes for our candy store, and it was a fun task.

My task was to put the pins through the box and then cut them off with wire cutters. After that, I would glue them on the backside because we wanted to shape them like fabric eggs. Those boxes became popular on the market. Then we also made other-style eggs, painted and decorated them to look like chocolate eggs, and stuck the pieces of Godiva chocolate on their roof. We would use them for the display and further decorate them with bright colors of chocolate on top, like pink, yellow, blue, etc.

Along with my artistic skills, my mom also taught me to use sewing machines and crochet. We had a little art project kit in which everything related to sewing and crocheting came in a little bag. I made several projects with the help of that kit, which was always fun and challenging at the same time.

I remember that when I was at Texas Tech, I took art history classes; I also remember back when I was nine years old, my mom bought me a Star Wars art kit, a box of markers, colors, papers, and other drawings. So, whenever I painted something, my mom would frame it and hang it in the playroom.

By doing these, my mom always inspired me to do better and keep improving my art skills. She wanted me to excel in those skills since she knew my interest in the arts and how neatly I would color. At the same time, we had other artistic hobbies, like making birdhouses and other simple projects from wood.

Chapter 8: Culinary Creativity and Family Traditions

I was eleven years old when my mom and I were convincing my father about the three huge pumpkins we bought, each weighing approximately sixty to seventy pounds. My mom wanted to decorate the front porch of our house with a big pumpkin, and she bought the other two for both El-Chico restaurants.

We reassured him that those pumpkins would not go to waste, and I remember him saying, "How are they not going to waste?"

My mom said, "Well, we will take the pumpkin seeds out and toast them. Then we will make pumpkin pies." We cooked our first batch of delicious pumpkin pies when I was six. They became very famous and liked by everyone. We reassured my dad by making him remember that. Then, my dad somehow agreed.

After some time, each pumpkin we got yielded a hundred pies, and we made three hundred pumpkin pies. I vividly remember when we were on our second pumpkin, my dad came and said, "You've all proven your point. Now, you don't need to finish this."

But we said, "No, we will finish this." We kept the fresh ones out in our store for sale, and we stored some of them in the freezer to enjoy later. We opened our store on Thanksgiving morning for a few hours and sold those fresh pumpkin pies to the people at Otto's, the restaurant. They asked if they could buy bread rolls, so we took special orders and baked bread rolls for them, which they liked so much. We were open from 9:00 a.m. to 11:30 a.m., and we sold dozens of bread rolls since they were very popular.

One random day in spring, I remember a man coming up to our door and telling us that he sold fur coats.

He said to my mom, "Patty, I hate to bother you, but by any chance, do you have any of your pumpkin pies left in the freezer? I am craving them, so I thought I should stop by and see if you have any left," and we had one left that my mom stored in the freezer. So, my mom gave that last pie to the man, and he really enjoyed it.

In the first ten years of our candy store, from 1981 to 1991, we did not stop experimenting with different chocolate recipes. As a result, we made our chocolate line, which was loved by everyone in the town. We experimented with different delicious recipes. Swiss Alp Truffle was one of them, and it was really flavorful. It was basically made up of chocolate and banana flavors and had a few other ingredients.

Second, we had fudge, which we made in the big copper kettles because copper kettles distribute the heat evenly throughout the pot simultaneously, with one part of it not getting hotter than the other. They were bigger, so we would need two adults to fill them until they were full. Usually, there were three sizes of copper kettles, of which we had the biggest one. The bottom of which would fit on one regular burner, but the pot was so wide that it would cover up all four burners. We would not be able to cook anything else on the other three burners because of the space the kettle took up.

We would make caramel and fudge from scratch and experiment with different recipes. We also had our own little secret ingredients that we would add to make our fudge smoother and silkier than usual. We tried our fudge with caramel, chocolate, cream, and so on.

Additionally, we would encounter unique requests from our customers. One day, a man came up with an empty jar. He told us that his mom sent this chocolate-filled jar to him. The chocolates were wrapped and looked like pickles, and he ate them all. Later, he got to know that some of the chocolates in that jar were for his brother-in-law as well, but he ate them all. So, he asked us if we could refill it with chocolate pickles, and he told us that the chocolates were not pickle-flavored; they were just milk chocolates shaped like pickles.

So, the only chocolate mold we had that would be close to those chocolates was a peanut mold. However, for the peanut mold, we would have to take two sides of the peanut and wrap it in green foil, and then he could pass it off as pickle chocolate. That idea worked, and we completed his request.

There were some other interesting requests, like when some customers would come and ask if they would like to have chocolate cut into pieces, put a ring inside one piece, and then put the chocolate back together. That would probably be for the engagement or anniversary gift, but we did not recommend that idea because it could go wrong, as the receiver would not be aware of the ring inside, and they could swallow it. However, at the end of the day, it was the customer's choice.

There were also the customers who wanted the ring to nestle between the chocolate and the paper cup so the receiver could see the ring, and that idea made sense to me as it had no harm. One day, we had a customer who wanted a necklace to put in the chocolate. He laid the chain under the chocolates and kept the diamond in the piece of chocolate; again, we would not recommend it, but it was up to the customer.

So, back to our Thanksgiving dinner, which we always spent at our home, and my mom would enjoy making turkey and other dishes. Our meals usually come from restaurants between lunch and dinner, so my mom rarely cooked throughout the year. So, on Thanksgiving, she would joke that it was her warmup for Christmas since she only cooked two meals a year.

For Thanksgiving, we tried making different sweet dishes and experimented with different cakes. When we would bake cakes in our candy store for the restaurant, we would utilize chocolates, some candies, and lemon slices to decorate the cakes. My best friend, David, and Ronnie would also help us bake cakes. I always had fun with them. However, when it comes to experimenting with new recipes and ideas, it would be just me and my mom. Sometimes, either Ronnie or David would help make chocolate; we had a bunch of flavors and colors. If someone wanted it special, we would make it for them. We would also experiment with cotton seed clusters in banana creams, normal cherry cordials, and orange and lemon creams. We also had large truffles, like Swiss Alp truffles, that served up to four people. They were each about the size of a baseball. There was also Mama Carter's fruitcake cookie recipe, which was really good. Making and experimenting with chocolates was always fun, but it was challenging and would take time.

It became our family tradition to always work in the candy store, even on holidays, when everyone else would enjoy it. My mom and I would go to the retail stores and buy our needed stocks. After the holidays, when our sales would get a bit slower, we could take a few breaks. Our busy season would start in September or October, and then it would go all the way through Valentine's Day, Easter, and Mother's Day. However, some customers would tell us to remind people that fathers like chocolate, too.

So, we would have a lot more busy nights in October, November, and December. My mom and I would work late in our store and prepare things for the next day. On Thanksgiving, I would help my mom, and then we had dinner together, followed by a rest. My dad would usually take a nap, while my mom and I would go back to the store to get any last-minute things done before Black Friday. It was never busier for us because a lot of people would go to the malls; however, the small businesses would be busier on Saturday, and then it was business as usual. On Christmas Eve, we had the most fun when people would come in for their last-minute gifts. I would enjoy that a lot; they would usually come at night after putting their kids to sleep. They would come in, shop, and get their coffee or tea. Most people would come to buy the stuff that Santa would bring to you. However, if people had their out-of-town guests arriving at the last minute, they would not have bought anything for them because they would never expect their guests to make it to their town. Since we were open, they would stop by and pick something up and say, "Okay, now this is better as it doesn't look like we forgot them. If we had to go to a big box store, they might feel we forgot them, so we are so glad your store is open for last-minute gifts." Then, after New Year's, business would slow down again. We had a bit of downtime, but not much, because we would need to start preparing everything for Valentine's.

Chapter 9: Celestial Encounters and Unanticipated Opportunities

Apart from opening the store, chocolate-making experiments, and shifting our store, we have encountered other interesting experiences over the years. In 1979, my mom and I took sailing lessons at Maxey Park, where we spent every week learning the ropes with James on a serene lake surrounded by a small island. The island, now deteriorating and shrinking over time, was a haven for ducks and geese.

During our lessons, everything went smoothly until it was time for our solo test. We set off confidently with James watching from the shore and camera in hand. However, the wind suddenly picked up that afternoon, catching us off guard. Our boat capsized, flipping side down, and my feet bungled in the rope. My mom and I found ourselves trapped under the boat. My initial thought was to remain calm and not panic.

When the boat capsized, my mom quickly untangled the rope from my feet, and we managed to escape to the ship's side. James watched anxiously from the shore, camera in hand, but he could not assist us since he couldn't swim and we were too far out. My mom reassured him, yelling that we were okay. James offered to get help; in the meantime, the instructor came over to James and said, "Swim on in. We will get the boat later," but my mom declined, saying we could handle it.

With James still motioning for us to return to shore, my mom and I stubbornly decided to continue our solo lesson. We flipped the boat back over, climbed aboard, and completed our solo test, determined to graduate from sailboat school - which we did!

My mom and I went to the local Oldsmobile dealership. We were standing in a line waiting to get autographs from the stars of the series who were retiring from The Batman TV series. Adam West was not there, but Bert Ward and Yvonne Craig, who played Robin and Batgirl, were.

While standing in line, my mom and I talked about inviting them to our restaurants for dinner. I told my mom not to forget to ask, and she said, "I won't forget, but be prepared for a no." When our turn came, we met them, got their autographs, and my mom invited them with the expectation of 'NO.'

However, to our surprise, they accepted our invitation and visited our restaurant for dinner. Bert Ward was dressed in a sports coat and slacks, while Yvonne wore a beautiful dress. It was around 9:00 at night, and after setting up the dinner table for them, we wanted to let them have their dinner. Therefore, when we started walking away from the table, they called us, saying, "Patty? Scott? Where do you think you are going?"

My mom said, "Well, we want you to enjoy your dinner time."

They said, "No, we came here to have dinner with you." Then, my mom and I sat with them and had dinner with Yvonne Craig and Bert Ward. We had an incredibly enjoyable experience with them; they were very interesting and down-to-earth. They told us they were still active in making cartoon series, books, and other educational things. They were there for a little over two hours, and that was a dinner I will never forget.

Moving forward, I was at our candy store in the Memphis Mall in the late nineties. It was Sunday, and I saw Gene Simmons from the band 'KISS' with his friends having dinner at the restaurant across the hall from the store. After finishing his dinner, he visited our candy store, and I recognized that he was Gene Simmons. I was shy but trying to be better and more talkative with customers. Also, I knew it was him, or at least I was ninety-nine percent sure.

We had a twenty-minute conversation, in which I observed him as a nice and fun man to talk to. After he left my store, I called my friend and told him everything, and he said, "You know what? Let me check." After which he called me in two weeks and said, "Guess who was in town two weeks ago and had a meal across the hall at Harrigan's on Sunday night? It was Gene Simmons." So that's how I met the famous American musician Gene Simmons.

Then again, in 2014, on Sunday night, we were in our restaurant, and the phone of the restaurant rang. My mom picked up the phone, and someone asked if we were open. My mom said yes, so they said, "Well, we are finishing up at a church with a little performance, so we are coming over for dinner." After a while, when they visited, it turned out that they were the Gatlin Brothers. They had a singing and performing session at church. It was surprising for us since we were not expecting any musicians to visit at that moment. As usual, they were nice and humble.

I've had the pleasure of meeting several musicians and celebrities, and my experiences have been overwhelmingly positive. Contrary to the stereotype that famous individuals can be rude and disappointing, I've found them humble, kind, and genuinely friendly. Each one has shown generosity and warmth, defying some people's negative expectations. These encounters have left a lasting impression on me, and I feel grateful to have met such down-to-earth and gracious individuals.

Another interesting encounter we had in San Francisco was the day after our chocolate school ended. My mom and I were walking down the street, where we met Stanley Marcus. My mom told him that she liked his store and everything he had done within it. We talked to him for about ten minutes.

So, meeting celebrities and famous people has always been a very exciting experience for me and my mom.

I recall a Tuesday morning at our small store in Memphis, where Heidi and I were working. A man walked in, and we offered to assist him. He explained that he needed to order some gift baskets. We asked about his preferences, suggesting options like coffee, tea, chocolate, or a variety.

He asked to borrow our phone so he could call and confirm the details quickly. After a brief conversation, he returned the phone and specified his order: one coffee-themed basket and two baskets with a combination of coffee, tea, chocolate, and candy.

We confirmed the order and asked when he needed the gift baskets. He shared his name, contact information, and pickup time. As he was on the phone earlier, I noticed he was wearing a bowl game ring from Texas Tech, hinting at a football connection. After finalizing the order, he thanked us and shared a surprising story. He revealed that he was a new assistant coach under Mike Leach and that morning, Coach Leach assigned him a special task. During their meeting, Coach Leach noticed he was the only one without a girlfriend or family and didn't want him to miss out on the Christmas spirit. So, he instructed him to order gift baskets from Otto's Granary, mentioning that if he had any questions, he could call back and speak with his assistant for guidance. We did not get a chance to meet Mike Leach then, but after that, I made deliveries to the football office a couple of times. It was late afternoon, so Mike Leach was the only staff member there.

Once, when I visited the football office for the delivery, two ABC announcers were closing the office door. One of them saw me and noticed a box filled with the little boxes from Godiva for coaches and assistant coaches.

One of the announcers came to me and said, "Hey, I am Coach Leach," and the other one introduced himself as Ruffin McNeil.

I gazed at them and said, "Sorry guys, I don't think so."

Then, one of them opened the door and talked to someone, yelling down the hall, "Hey, Mikey, you have a delivery." Then he turned to me and said, "Mikey will be here in a minute to receive his delivery, he is back there cleaning up."

After a little while, Mikey came out, and to my surprise, he was the coach, Mike Leach. I was excited, and we talked for about ten to fifteen minutes about football and basketball. He also asked me about our store. I had always found them really nice and polite.

These coaches would also visit my parents' restaurant from time to time. Coach Bobby Knight once visited our restaurant with his friend Coach Larry Hayes (head baseball coach). They had a great time at my parents' restaurant as well.

Also, Coach Marsha Sharp (head Lady Raiders basketball coach) had visited my store several times. She was always nice, having food in our restaurants with her colleagues. I would hear someone saying, "Hey, Scott." I would look around and see Coach Sharp waving at me, and then I stepped over and talked with her for a few minutes.

After Coach Marsha Sharp retired from coaching, Texas Tech hired Coach Kristi Curry (head Lady Raiders basketball coach). She had also visited my store a few times and told the man in charge of promotions that she thought we would be the perfect fit for the Kiss Cam sponsor. So, in every home game, the winner of the Kiss Cam would receive a pound box of Godiva chocolates with a gift certificate for fajitas for two at my parents' restaurant.

Chapter 10: Memorable Experiences

We also started making commercials for our candy store when I was thirteen years old. I remember I was nominated to be in our commercial, but sometimes, some other workers of our candy store would also participate in the commercials for our candy store. At first, I used to be shy, but with the support team's help, I could do it very well.

Even though the act was only to walk up a ramp, enter the candy store, and look at the chocolate boxes on the counter, it was changed later, and I would be behind the case. I became very good at it with time and practice, and we had to do only one or two takes.

I remember we were making an ad for our candy store in which we had a statue, and I had to set it down, turn it, and look up. I wasn't doing it as fast as it needed to be done, so one of our ad executives helped me. She stood behind the cameraman and gave me instructions like, "Set the statue down," "Turn the statue to the left," "Stop," "Now look up," and I followed her commands. It was very helpful and fun.

In 2019, we found a company for custom ugly sweaters. They were called ugly sweaters because they were a style. However, when I wore them for commercials, they would look good, yet they would fall into the ugly category. On one of those sweaters, we designed the Otto Man of our candy store and the building, which many people liked. Hence, over the years, there have been a lot of exciting activities at our candy store.

We had several Texas Tech cheerleaders working in our store, and working with them was really fun and exciting. They had an excellent work ethic and would also give us ideas for our displays. I remember I wanted to make my background display with puzzles, but it would take a lot of time to solve the puzzles and glue them to the foam core board to create a perfect background display. So, one of our Texas Tech cheerleaders suggested, "You can give us a to-do list before you go out, and we will finish the tasks on it, and then we will do the puzzles."

I liked that idea, so I did it and went out with my friend. I remember him saying, "Well, you know your workers will probably stop as soon as you walk out the door; they would just be good off and do the puzzle." So, I called my candy store and asked them, "How much of the puzzle did you get done to complete it so that I can glue it together tomorrow?"

They replied, "Honestly, we just finished the to-do list; we haven't had time to open it yet." It proved that everybody who worked at the candy store had been a good worker and always had a good work attitude.

I remember my mom buying me a huge puzzle of 'Michelangelo's Sistine Chapel,' which I had worked on for two years. Since I would not have much time to solve the puzzle in the fall and winter, I would do it during the summer. The puzzle consisted of eight thousand pieces three feet wide and nine feet long. But after two years, I decided to take it to Otto's. We had an Armani shipment coming in, and the complete puzzle would provide an excellent background for it. But we had to complete it before the shipment came in. So, during the summertime, we had a big table, and I had to put cardboard on it to extend it to make it longer and wider. The table had eight seats, which was not big enough for the puzzle. So, I had to make it bigger.

Additionally, if customers came into the store, they were welcome to help and put some pieces in if they wanted to. There were a few that did, but there was a lady who had two children. They used to come to the store once a week and buy a piece of chocolate. When they saw us doing the puzzle, they started coming every day after school to buy a piece of chocolate and check the progress of the puzzle.

In the middle of solving the puzzle, we received an order from Fitz and Floyd, so we had to complete the puzzle soon. We needed a table to display the order from Fitz and Floyd and the complete background of the puzzle for the display. Hence, the puzzle became a project for us.

For our luck, four Texas Tech cheerleaders worked at the store on their day off that year. One of their boyfriends, who was a Texas Tech cheerleader, also worked at the store. He came into the store to get some chocolate while his girlfriend was in class; she wasn't working that day. So, he sat down to work on a puzzle. Two hours later, I saw him still working on the puzzle. I walked over with a cup of coffee, and he said, "I know I hate puzzles. I don't do puzzles, and I'm not working today, but I'm not leaving till I finish this section."

He stayed for a couple more hours, totaling around four hours, until he completed the section of the puzzle he was working on. The next day, it was Sunday afternoon, and we were trying to finish the puzzle to move it. Suddenly, we started to get sleepy, so one of the workers decided to make chamomile tea. Later, we realized that chamomile tea is good for relaxation, and you should never have it while working. So, Julie said that she had to make us a new pot of tea, i.e., green tea. We had tea, and that day, we worked late until the puzzle was solved. We took it out into the hall and attached it with a foam core board. Then we put a drop cloth down and carefully glued them with spray glue. We made sure that there were no bumps or bubbles on it. We left it for an hour to dry and completed the other work. When it completely dried, we placed it upright upon one of our workers' suggestions and left it till morning.

However, the next day, the puzzle started losing shape and sagging when we came to it. The bubbles began to appear in it, and we could not stick them back. It also did not fit because it slipped overnight. So, we had to have a machete knife with a long blade to cut the puzzle off of the foam core board. Then we took it in small sections and reglued it onto a new foam core board, which worked well.

We had another idea: to use a metal square, so we started the first corner of the puzzle because that would get us about two feet down in each direction. However, we got about four or five feet down, but the pieces did not match together, and there was so little space left that we could not even force the pieces together. So, we reglued the puzzle and started again, but this time, we did it without a square. We glued it all back and put several coats of glue on it. After it dried, we were able to stand it up behind the display. Then, we moved it with us from Memphis Place Mall, and we had to take it with us back to the Granary; it was challenging to take it over to the granary, KO's Carol, which used to be the dining room, and the ceiling was sloped at an angle. We placed the Sistine Chapel on the ceiling and mounted them with mirror clips. The problem we faced was getting a three-by-nine-foot puzzle into the Carol while having exposed wooden beams inside. So, we had to take it carefully because we could not bend it. We used two ladders, a couple of dust mops, and a broom on which we had put a towel to cover the end of the broom. We had to go up in the attic and come across the ceiling with it. We did not want any scratches or damage to the puzzle, so we did not land it on the rafters.

To take the puzzle across, we had a person on a ladder and another person between the ladders on the floor with the dust mop holding it up while someone moved the ladder over and down a little further so we could get the puzzle up. Finally, when we assembled the whole puzzle, we found that one piece was missing. So, we took a small section of the puzzle up the hall to the copy store, made a black-and-white copy, and enlarged it to the correct size. We did the whole thing, then moved and put it up there. We had the kiosk inside our Memphis Place Mall store. I thought doing it piece by piece would be easier than working on the entire thing at once. We had it inside our Memphis Place Mall store, but when we moved to the granary, we used the parts of it in the corral and the other parts in the tea gallery. We also utilized the four mirrored columns and the top part of the canopy before the entrance of the coffee room. So that puzzle was interesting to do.

One day, Heidi and I were unpacking a large order of Charming Tails with over 100 unique items to sort through. We sat in a cozy vignette area, surrounded by bookcases, a coffee table, and a rug, carefully checking off each item on the list. The names of the Charming Tails were quite romantic, such as "I Love You," "You're Very Sweet," "You Mean the World to Me," and "Love Chocolate." Our coworker walked by, seemingly distracted but listening in on our conversation. He teased us, saying it didn't sound like we were working but instead conversing. To prove him wrong, I asked him to read off the top five lines on the list. He did, and his expression changed. He returned the list, saying, "Never mind, never mind. Go back to... uh, cleaning up for customers." He realized the Charming Tails were themed for various holidays like Valentine's Day, Easter, Mother's Day, and everyday occasions.

Chapter 11: Our Chocolate Legacy

Our chocolate legacy would start with the smell of chocolate. My mom and I have always loved chocolate. Dark chocolate was always our favorite, and white chocolate was our least favorite. However, companies added a hint of vanilla flavoring or a touch of vanilla flavoring to the white chocolate, which would taste delicious. As said earlier, we started making chocolate at home as a hobby when I was six. That habit grew into a hobby that we enjoyed and would always have fun doing. My friends would come over and stay for the weekend, and we would work on the fun projects in the evening.

Sometimes I would be up late working on making chocolate suckers and different pieces of chocolate, but chocolate making has always been a passion of mine and my mom. Our passion made the most beautiful memories for our family and friends.

My mom enrolled us in the chocolate school when I was ten, which made me more enthusiastic about chocolate. When I was in my twenties, we got a few phone calls at different times when some schools wanted to know if there was someone who could visit their school and take a session about chocolate making. I was the one nominated and was a bit nervous at first because I've always been the shy one. However, going up and talking about chocolate to a group was interesting. There were students of every age who would ask me different questions about chocolate and how it's made. I enjoyed those sessions. Our chocolate legacy is full of exciting moments. I remember the truffle we came up with, in which we put a secret ingredient to keep it fresh. We kept it in the freezer, took it out, and cut it, and it still tasted fresh even after two years. The interesting fact about that truffle was that it was the size of a baseball. We did different experiments at home to see how long something would last and still be fresh, like the chuck we made to sell in the store. We made it daily, but it never stayed around that long because it sold quickly. It was always nice to experiment with chocolate.

Then, going through the years, we focused on the chocolate store, along with my studies. The first ten years in which we made our chocolate line were challenging yet fun. It doesn't matter in which industry you're in; to succeed, you must work hard. Making chocolate is not as easy as whipping cream. It is an art that takes time, passion, and talent. Tempering chocolate has to be done correctly if you want a good result. Moreover, when making chocolate molds, you need to tap them to ensure you have the chocolate in them. Before it starts cooling down, you need to ensure that it has no bubbles or air gaps in the mold.

Everything is about timing. If you wait too long, it gets hard, and bubbles form. But my mom and I always enjoyed what we did at the store. Waiting on the customer was my mom's least favorite, so she would rather be in the store, and I had to agree with her so I would rather be in the store waiting on customers. However, there are many things that we have learned from different people over the years about chocolates. My mom and I would work daily together; we always loved it. But she unexpectedly passed away in 2016 at the age of seventy-seven, and my dad passed away eighteen days after her at the age of ninety-one. It was December 1st, 2016, at 01:15 a.m., when my mom passed, and on December 19th, 2016, my dad passed away. I kept a positive attitude, believing everything happens for the best at the right time. My mom had been diagnosed with early-onset dementia five weeks before she passed.

My friends have told me that I was fortunate because I didn't have to go through things that some others had to go through with this disease. So, there is always a bright side, which is a little hard to find, but you can find one. There is always one there.

My mom and I enjoyed the times when we would go to the market, which was always a learning experience. We also visited the fancy food show in New York, which was an exciting experience. On our trip to London, we would find markets and visit them to explore chocolate-making products.

So, after the death of my parents, I had the chocolate store and the restaurant, along with the online sales that we started. We planned to start on our website, which was a tour of the stores. It had been for many years; we were changing it and adding a shopping cart to sell online. That was always challenging because a website takes almost as much time as a physical store. So, having my parents' restaurant, website, and physical store was the toughest. Well, in December 2019, I was thinking about closing the restaurant or letting someone else take over the franchise. Instead, I wound up closing it and selling the property, focusing on the store and website.

However, time passed, and good times came for our store when COVID-19 came around. Lubbock closed in March, but we had food, coffee beans, tea, chocolates, and some of our gourmet salsas. So, we kept our sales going and entered the essentials category.

We thought we had to do curbside, but we could still go to work, open the store, ship orders, and take things out to people curbside. During that timeframe, we were going to do a little remodel on the store, but things happened that pushed the remodel back. So, we wound up not reopening and letting customers back into the store until September 2022. But at least we had the online store.

Coming to my artistic experiences in my chocolate legacy, my mom always encouraged my art since I was very good at painting and drawing when I was five or six. I would color with colored pencils, and I always did it neatly. My mom would take my darlings, frame them, and hang them on the walls. I remember James putting a giant bulletin board in one of our halls, but he painted it white, so it was the same color as the wall. But with the drawing and painting, it looked colorful and beautiful. We could always stick my paintings up there with the thumbtack. Apart from my artistic and chocolate-making experiences, we would also enjoy cooking in our store and restaurant. We would cook a special dinner on Sunday, and my dad would come home and eat. Then, he would go back to the restaurant later that evening.

One thing that my mom and I always wanted to do was write a book, but we never got to it. We always thought this would be an exciting story about chocolates and art. It has been forty-three years since the store opened.

When my parents passed, my mom was 71, and my dad was 91, and neither one had retired. They worked to the very end, but we all loved what we did. So, I don't intend to go anywhere anytime soon.

I still have plans to get started making our West Texas Gold chocolates. I do miss my mom, and I remember the advice my friend gave me at the time of my mom's death. She said my mom was never really gone; she was somewhere else and watching down over me. I listened to my friend's advice and never used the past tense for my mom. For example, there are several customers to whom I tell them that a particular chocolate is mine and my mom's favorite, and someone comes up to me and taps on my shoulder a little bit later and asks, "Are you okay?"

I say, "Yeah, I'm fine."

They confusedly replied, "What? You realize it's been three or six months since she passed away?"

To which I reply, "I know. Do you mean it was? No, it is, and so I was told by a good friend that I should always,

always, and never use past tense. So, therefore, I'm staying with it." Growing up, I also had three dogs, of which we gave a couple to my grandmother and then one to a friend. Since then, I never really had time for my dogs because I had to go to school and then the store. My parents have two El Chico restaurants in Lubbock and Otto's Granary Restaurant. We then moved to the Otto's attic store, then the Otto Memphis small store, so I could not spend time with my dog.

But after my parents passed, I did go, and it took me three months to pick the breed and then three months to find the dog I wanted. Finally, I got Bella, a tricolor little Cavalier King Charles Spaniel. Later, I added another dog named Lady Godiva. Then, my great aunt came and teased me, "When are you getting a third?" I said no, I am fine with two. She said, "But you always do things in threes." We were messing around and looking at the breeder's website, and I saw a puppy, but two weeks later, he was still available. So, I got him too and ended up with three again, and they are all a lot of fun.

I spend quality time with my dogs; they all have spots, like chairs, sofas, etc., where they like to lay.

Chapter 12: Interesting Stories

My parents would park a car at each end of the driveway, making a safe boundary so Ronnie, David, and I could play in the middle of the driveway without getting into the street. Since it was a circular driveway and we had big wheels that we would ride around, I remember one day that we were racing, and we tried to stop, but we slipped into the hubcap. We hit the hubcap of my dad's car and put it back in; luckily, he didn't notice. However, my mom saw it, so we opted just to see if he noticed it and how long it took him to notice it. It might have been a good six months or a year later, but I was still unsure that he noticed it.

James made some little stop signs and yield signs placed in the driveway when we were riding around, which was always a fun experience. Then, there was a lot across the street from our house, and a man who used to live in the neighborhood sold it to my parents for $2,000. When the street debt ended, we got a place to play that was safe and nearby in the neighborhood. We did not have to walk several blocks to the park to play. So, we would go to the lot and play Frisbee. We would take the golf clubs and practice driving the golf balls because they had a fence at the end of them, and we would play baseball there as well. So that was handy.

But I remember my mom and I going on bike rides when I was younger. She had a 10-speed, and I had a dirt bike then. It was a candy apple red with yellow grips and a pad. We would ride probably about 12–14 blocks from the house and would come back, and we got less than halfway. My mom would say, "Here, just give it a try," instead, she wound up on the small bicycle, and I wound up on the 10-speed for the rest of the ride home. It was tough and funny at the same time. She got a laugh out of it, and she said, "Okay, next time, we'll just take both 10-speeds instead of the small and big."

Next to the restaurant was a concrete culvert that would stay dry most of the time. Because of that, we could come down to the restaurant. We could bring roller skates with us, and we would take a broom in a slipping area to make sure there weren't any rocks so we could go roller skate down there. So, it was a nice and safe area because it was blocked off at one end, so cars could not drive up there.

There was another time when it had been snowing outside, and my mom and I parked out back and went into the restaurant's kitchen. Our staff was busy doing their chores, so to lighten up the moment, my mom went out, and at first, I didn't know what she was doing. She walked in with a snowball in her hand and lightly tossed it towards the feet of one of the cooks. They looked at her shockingly and didn't know how to react. Then, my mom smiled, and everyone started laughing.

I also remember hearing the story because it happened a year before I was born. When my parents first opened the restaurant, there were two cooks, Armando and Henry. So, one day, one of them was trying to put the bucket of oatmeal with water above the doorway. He was trying to get the other one, and at the same time, my dad walked through wearing a three-piece suit and a bucket with oatmeal and water dumped on him. My dad did not get angry, but he just told him they didn't need to play jokes like that at work. Then he came home and changed.

Another incident like this happened with a manager years later. I remember when the managers came for lunch, and at the same time, there was a painting going on in the restaurant. The painter had put the ladder in the back closet and left it open. He just set the can of paint on it and didn't close the lid correctly. At the same time, the manager went out there to get some towels from the shelf, and he moved the ladder without realizing the bucket of paint had a loose lid on it. The whole one gallon of brown paint spilled all over his suit. The manager got unhappy and mad at the painter. He was not a happy camper. The suit was poorly stained and could not even be sent to the cleaners, so my mom bought him a new one. I remember he was very unhappy with the painter since there was no reason the painter should have left a can without labeling it. He should have put it down securely. But at any rate, things like that happen.

One day, I came home from school to lunch at the restaurant and sat with my mom, talking about random stuff. All of a sudden, we saw the manager running by the window. And we got up from our place to see what was happening there. A few minutes later, he came back. A guy walked behind him, and when he approached the man, who was much bigger than the manager, he said, "Please don't hit me."

The manager said, "I will not, but you come back and do the dishes." He came back and did the dishes. When he walked in, the police came out too and talked to him. The understanding was made that he would stay and do dishes till after lunch, and then he would get to leave and go home. So, my mom and dad told Armando, our manager, that it would be better to let him leave and not chase him down. Since you never know if he was armed or not, that was a safer step to take, and I agreed with that. Since I have heard stories of people who will follow someone, unfortunately, that person has a gun or a knife. At the same time, I don't know many people who move faster than a bullet, so to be on the safe side, you should just let them go.

Moving forward, my mom and I would always love to go on trips. So, whether it be the fancy food show or market in LA or the market in Chicago, we would catch a flight and go there to spend time at the market and enjoy the sights.

My dad would like to go on motorcycle trips with his friends, sometimes with one or sometimes with a group of friends. He went to the four corners of the United States: San Diego, Washington State, Maine, and New Hampshire. He ought to look at Key West and then go back again. He was in his early eighties when he did that. In his mid-eighties, he went to Alaska on his motorcycle with one friend. He always enjoyed his motorcycle trips, and we always encouraged them. We'd have a map of the restaurant, and he would usually call us daily to tell us his location. And we would mark that place on the map. It was written on the top of the map: *WHERE is KEN TODAY?*

There have been challenges through the years since there was always a busy time and a slow time in our restaurants. The good thing about the slow load time was that we would get time to change our displays, do restocking if needed, etc. I have always worked with both my parents in the restaurant, the El Chico restaurant, the Otto's granary restaurant, and the Otto candy store. I remember my mom passing away on December 16, 2015, after Thanksgiving. She fell at a restaurant outside Fort Worth, and they airlifted her back to Fort Worth. A friend came over and met me at the house that night and talked to the doctor in the emergency room, and they could decipher more about what they were talking about. They booked me on a flight the next morning to Dallas, where I arrived at five in the morning, a day after my mom went there.

The day my mom went there, the medical staff thought it was a broken hip, which turned out to be a broken neck. My great-aunt, who was with her, had her cell phone. My mom looked at my great-aunt and said, "Joy, what do you think you're doing?"

My aunt said, "I'm going to call Scott."

"No, Kenneth is in the hospital. Scott is working for the holidays. He is keeping an eye on the restaurant and the store. He's busy. You can call him later," said my mom.

"But I need to call him." Aunt Joy insisted.

"No, it's just a broken hip; no big deal; you can call him later." My mom said, Then, in a few minutes, Aunt Joy tried to sneak my mom's phone back. My mom caught her saying, "Joy, are you trying to call Scott again? I already told you it's a broken hip; it's no big deal. He's busy. Do not disturb him right now." And then later, she went into a coma.

When I reached there a day later, I found her in a coma. She was in good spirits beforehand, even though she was in pain. I believed that everything happens at the right time, making it a lot easier to deal with things. I was close to my mom, and I still am, but I remember Ann always saying, "Just remember, they're never really gone. They're just somewhere different from this world," and I never used past tense for them.

The hospital shifted my mom back to Lubbock in an ambulance. We followed her back. When they pulled up in front of this other building, they got out and told us they were sorry. She just passed.

After my mom's passing at the age of seventy-seven, my uncle, who was my mom's brother from Arkansas, and my cousin drove out here for the funeral. Some of my other cousins also came to the funeral. We went over to Tahoka, about thirty minutes from Lubbock. I remember it was raining and snowing that day. About two and a half weeks later, my dad passed unexpectedly at the age of ninety-one. It was also raining and snowing during his funeral. He had a massive heart attack in the doctor's office. The last thing he said was a joke he told another man and laughed at. After all that, my parents' goal was to hit 50 years in the restaurant, and they were a little short of that. Since they passed in December 2016, September 2019 was about to be their 50th year, and I kept it till the end of December 2019.

I was debating if I wanted to renew the franchise agreement in January. I was on the fence back and forth, but a costly piece of equipment went out through the roof. It was going to cost at least $25,000 to replace it. I talked to someone at corporate, and they said, "Well, in the next two years, you're probably going to have at least two more big expenses like that, if not more expensive. So, if you want to get out of the restaurant business, this is a good time."

I completed my parents' 50 years at the restaurant and decided this was a good time. My great aunt and uncle in Arkansas agreed with my decision and said, "You have two angels up there sending you a message that it's time to gather us from business." Then, COVID-19 rolled around a few months later, so it was the right time to get out with everything in early 2020.

Moving forward, I would like to share my puppy's story, which is also very interesting. So, I grew up with three or four dogs but have not had a dog since 1984. In 2017, I spent three months deciding what kind of dog I wanted. My great-aunt and I talked in December because she stayed here for Christmas and said, "Well, you need a dog?"

I said, "Yes, that's what I was thinking, too." I fully intended to get one and decided to wait for one or two years to get a second one. However, it did not exactly happen that way. I got one dog, and it took me three months to pick out the breed.

Then, I had my cousin's wedding towards the end of May, and my dog came at the end of May, the day after we got back in town for my cousin's wedding. I picked her up; her name was Bella, and she was a very good little dog. I enjoyed her company. She was definitely in charge of all of her brothers and sisters. They were the oldest and the smallest, but they would all listen to her. She was approximately seven pounds lighter than her sister or twelve pounds lighter than her other sister and brother. But they all paid attention to Bella.

After having Bella for about a month and a half, we walked on a Sunday morning. Someone had abandoned a little Chiweenie over my gate. Since I had built a little fence around the front of the yard in the spring before I had a dog, I wondered if there were kids or dogs in the front yard while it was snowing. They could come to the fence for shelter. I thought the fence was just for safety.

It was about 10 feet off the street, and the fence would be so far away to be on the safe side. So, we named the little puppy Charlie and kept him with me for a week or two. He would usually be on Aunt Joy's lap, and Bella would be on her lap. One day, I picked him up and put him on my lap, and my throat started closing up in thirty seconds. I discovered I was allergic to his breed, so I found a good home for him. Then, a football season was rolling around, and I would feel guilty to leave Bella at home alone since she got used to a friend. So, I got Lady Godiva for Bella. So, there were two of them together. Then, when Aunt Joy came to Thanksgiving, she said, "Aren't you getting the third?"

I said, "Nope, I'm good with two."

She said, "We always do things in threes."

I said, "Yeah, but I'm good with two." Well, we were Fabiutwo from the breeder, and we saw St. Nicholas, and two weeks later, he was still there. So, I caved and got him.

Chapter 13: Family Memories

I believe everything happens for the best and at the right time. My Mom's diagnosis of early dementia came five weeks before her demise. Though I lost my mother, I believe that it was a blessing in disguise. A lot of people told me that the stages of dementia kept getting worse, and I was lucky that I did not have to go through them. I was relieved that my Mom had not had to suffer from the disease.

At the death of my Mom, the family members, cousins, and friends who were not in contact with each other came together. Everyone called each other to pass the news of my Mom's death. At her funeral, everyone arrived, and it was a kind of reunion for all of them. They are still together, a positive omen on my Mom's side. Moreover, as I said earlier, I was relieved that my mother had gone to the happy place, and she would still watch me take care of my candy store and restaurants.

Two weeks after my Mom's death, my father also passed away, and it was the Christmas season. My great-aunt came, and I spent Christmas with her. She said that if my father were alive, she would be at her home celebrating Christmas alone. Though my parents were not present, we celebrated Christmas with a couple who were also my employees. It was a soothing and happy Christmas. We had gifts for each other, and it all made it comforting. Everyone knows that the Christmas season is the best time of the year. People come, meet each other, exchange gifts, and make happy memories together. It was a little different at my home since we got to eat our Mom's cooked meal. It is humorous, but my Mom would cook only two times a year, once at Thanksgiving and then on the sacred occasion of Christmas. Thanksgiving would become a warm-up time for my Mom. We had our restaurants, so my Mom didn't have to cook. We would also check the quality of the meals by having them for our lunch and dinner.

My Dad would joke around with us while my Mom prepared to cook turkey. He would say to my Mom, "Are you shooting the turkey up again?" Or if someone at a restaurant asked him what he was having for Christmas dinner, he would say, "Well, my wife and son made a drunk turkey for me."

My Mom had a different way of filling the turkey with different flavors. She would use needles to inject different flavors, like apricot or schnapps, depending upon the liqueur in the turkey to keep it moist and tender. Sometimes, we would decorate the top of the turkey with pineapple rings. I would help my Mom by filling the needles with flavors. It was always a good time making turkey with my Mom.

When I was young, I would go on different trips with my Mom and Dad. In summer, we visited our Grandma, who lived in Arkansas. Once, when we visited her, my Mom and I decided to go back on a scenic route, so we talked to our Dad, and he agreed. We went through Oklahoma, covered up Colorado until the lower part of Oklahoma, and back to Texas. We enjoyed beautiful views; it was a heartwarming journey with my Mom and Dad. I remember my grandfather in Arkansas bought my Dad a motorhome. James fixed up the insides and built new cabinets and upholstery on the seats. We would go on trips in that motorhome, and my Mom and I would play cards while my Dad would drive. We had incredible trips in the motorhome except the last one. The door did not close properly, and on our way, all the back dust aired inside our motorhome. It was all messy and dirty when my Mom cleaned it once. But again, the dust came inside from somewhere, and we spent our entire trip cleaning the dust till we reached back to Lubbock. My Mom said, "This is our last trip in this motorhome," and then my Dad sold it.

I vividly remember a plane memory when I was 12. We were at American Airlines, and they gave us cards. So, my grandmother and I played, and it was fun. She sat with her back against the window, and the light from the window shone through the cards. I could see the numbers on her cards, and this way, I beat her seven to eight times in a row, and she said, "You are good at it; you have beaten me eight times in a row." But then I told her I could see the numbers on your card, and she laughed at my naughtiness. Next time, she hid her cards, but I beat her again, and then I realized I was actually good at it.

There was another epic memory of a plane from about 1982 when I was on a plane with my Mom going to California. I looked up at the plane's ceiling and saw the sky. I knew how sensitive it was. If I had screamed or spoken loudly, there would have been panic in the plane. So, I slowly told my Mom, and she also did not panic and handled the matter calmly. She called the air hostess and whispered in her ear. The air hostess looked up and saw a crack in the ceiling of a plane, and she immediately went to the pilot. The plane circled back to the airport and landed slowly, and then they switched our plane. However, a lady on the plane, who seemed to be in her fifties, figured out what was happening and started screaming, "WE ARE GOING TO DIE." The attendants handled her. Seeing her, I thought I was a 12-year-old kid and stayed calm, but that lady could not.

I remember I was on a flight with my Mom in the early to mid-1980s. I almost always get the window seat. So, my Mom and I talked about our trip and ideas for Otto's Granary; the flight was at least 6 hours or more. Suddenly, the lady sitting in front of me said, "Look! UFO!" We quickly raised the shade, and an unusual aircraft flew beside us. The pilot turned and waved at us. His helmet looked like an outer space helmet, and then he zipped off and disappeared out of sight.

This happened years before the F-117 Nighthawk was introduced to the public. It was doing a test flight when it flew by the commercial airliner we were on.

At the end of my book, I would like to talk a little about the great love story of my parents.

My mom used to work for a man named Mr. Smith. He would often tell her about a nice man named Ken, saying they would get along really well. However, before they could meet, my mom fell ill and was hospitalized. Mr. Smith visited her in the hospital and asked how she was doing. She told him she was recovering and would be back at work on Monday.

He replied, "That's great to hear." Then, he pointed to a man standing in the doorway and said, "By the way, that's Ken, the man I've been telling you about."

But he didn't introduce them properly at that time.

Six months later, on New Year's Eve, Ken called my mom and asked her to go out that evening. She accepted the invitation. They had a great time, and he proposed. She went home and called Mr. Smith at 2 a.m. to share the news.

He joked, "I hope you said yes!"

Then she called her mother, Granny, to tell her about the engagement. Granny immediately called Uncle Dan, saying, "Your sister just got engaged to a man only a few years younger than me! Talk to her and meet this man, then report back to me!"

They were concerned because there was a 14-year age difference between my mom and dad. Despite this, they got married on February 3, 1968, after getting engaged in December 1967.

A week before their wedding day, the most dangerous incident occurred when my mom and dad visited one of my uncles. My mom was wearing a red jacket, unaware of the potential danger that there was a bull in the pin next to the horse area. A bull began charging towards the fence where my mom was standing. Thankfully, someone quickly pulled her to safety and gave her a different coat, warning her that wearing red around a bull wasn't wise.

Sadly, they passed away just 18 days apart in December 2016. However, they had a long and happy life together.

My parents' love story is proof of the fact that true love can conquer all, even time. Despite what others may say about whirlwind romances being 'Hollywood magic,' my parents proved that you can get engaged on the first date, get married a month later, and enjoy a long and happy marriage. They were together for almost 48 years, never separated or divorced.

In the early days of their relationship, my dad would surprise my mom with flowers every Friday. They had a special dinner at my aunt's house, where my great aunt and uncle mentioned the opportunity to buy an El Chico franchise in Lubbock. Without telling my mom or uncle, my dad took their savings and invested in the franchise the very next week. This bold move led to their move from Dallas to Lubbock and the start of our family business.

Their love story is a reminder that true love can lead to a lifetime of happiness and adventure. And for our family, it's a legacy that we cherish to this day.

Chapter 14: Football Story

I have a collection of many exciting stories that we experienced throughout our childhood, from making chocolates to art and sports. This chapter has a fascinating story waiting for you to read and enjoy! I share this story in the loving memory of my dearest friend.

Growing up, one of my best friends from high school attended Texas A&M, while I went to Texas Tech after graduating. He later moved back to Lubbock and started his own business. We would always participate in the Texas Tech vs. Texas A&M football games together in Lubbock.

For the last 12 years, Texas A&M was in the Big 12 conference, and we typically played football against each other every other year, with a few back-to-back exceptions. We faced off around eight times in football over those 12 years, but I might be slightly off. One constant was that my friend David would always join me for the Texas Tech vs. Texas A&M games. He'd wear his Texas A&M hat or sweater and cheer for them until, in his opinion, they started making mistakes. Even then, he'd continue to support them while appreciating good plays by either team.

The most exciting part of the story was that over 12 years of football, David attended seven to eight home games where Texas Tech played against Texas A&M in Lubbock. In every one of those games, Texas A&M was favored to win, sometimes by a wide margin. While Texas Tech had an excellent team, they were often underestimated. I wasn't surprised when we won, but David was! And it wasn't just football - when basketball season rolled around, we played against Texas A&M in Lubbock 12 times, with six games each for men's and women's basketball. David was always there to cheer on his Aggies, while I proudly supported the Red Raiders.

David attended at least 10 of the 12 men's and 10 of the 12 women's basketball games between Texas Tech and Texas A&M, and incredibly, A&M lost every time.

One day, before a game, I met a man in a store who told me, "Scott, there's no way we'll win tonight. We'll lose big, and the whole team is leaving for the pros at the end of the year."

He mentioned they had a chance if someone on their team was injured, like the entire starting lineup. I shared the story about my friend David, who always seemed to bring bad luck to A&M. David was sitting behind me and overheard the conversation. He put his hand on my shoulder, patted me, and said, "Keep him!" And sure enough, A&M lost again. This happened at least ten times, with David attending ten men's and women's basketball games and A&M losing every single one.

That's not all - David attended at least seven football games between Texas Tech and Texas A&M over 12 years, with A&M losing every time! I joked that if he called someone at A&M, they might pay him to stay away from the games. Interestingly, there was one game where A&M

finally won, but David didn't attend because it coincided with his daughter's birthday. I'm not saying I'm superstitious, but the coincidence is striking! It's as if David's presence was a charm of good luck for Texas Tech.

I forgot to mention that the year Texas A&M's basketball team went pro after the season. After one of the games, David suddenly remembered the football game I attended at Texas A&M the previous fall.

I confirmed I was there, and he shared that he had taken his family to the game. David shared a humorous anecdote about an A&M vs. Texas Tech game. He remembered A&M leading by several touchdowns, but Texas Tech staged a dramatic comeback. David claimed he left the game in the late third quarter, joking that his departure secured A&M's victory. According to David, if he had stayed until the end, Texas Tech would have won. He quipped that by leaving early and exiting A&M property, he prevented Texas Tech's potential win. Ironically, A&M won by just three points. David jokingly took credit for the win, saying, "The only reason A&M won was that I left early."

My dad would often tease David about going to the games with me, saying, "You're taking my seat!" since my dad preferred to watch the games on TV at a restaurant or at home to avoid the crowds. But David would jokingly respond, "Oh no, that's fine! Your son thinks I bring good luck for Texas Tech and bad luck for Texas A&M! I'd chime. I'm not superstitious, but look at the facts! How can you argue with the evidence?" It became a lighthearted and humorous exchange between us, with David's attendance seemingly coinciding with Texas Tech's victories and Texas A&M's losses. "The games speak for themselves - whenever you're there, Texas Tech wins; otherwise, they lose."

I remember my friend's courageous battle with rare brain cancer. Despite being given only two months to live, he defied the odds and lived for two years, making the most of his time with his loved ones. As a professor, he'd often take his kids to concerts on Thursdays and return early Monday mornings for classes. Before one of the football games, he told me he was going back for more cancer treatment, but when I suggested we skip the game and rest at home, he insisted on joining me, saying, "Don't dare give those tickets to anyone else! I'm going with you to the Texas Tech vs. University of Texas game." Despite having surgery on Wednesday, he was his usual self on Saturday, and no one could even tell that he was ill. His determination and spirit were truly inspiring.

The class he taught at Texas Tech was the final hurdle before med school, and he'd say, "My class is straightforward - if you do your homework, you'll pass. If you don't, you'll still pass." But he'd emphasize that when it comes to doctors, we want those who do their homework and research, not those who don't. So, his goal was to give students willing to put in the effort a chance to succeed and get into med school.

David was an exceptional friend who left us too soon and is deeply missed.

Chapter 15: Memories

Surviving the 1970 Lubbock Tornado

In May 1970, my mom returned home from the hospital on 8 May, just three days after giving birth to me via cesarean section. On 11 May, a devastating tornado struck Lubbock, Texas. My mom was home alone with me, rocking me in the living room. A neighbor offered shelter in their cellar, but she declined, fearing the steep stairs would exacerbate her recent surgery.

Instead, she called my dad at the restaurant, expressing concern about the storm. He reassured her it was just a thunderstorm. However, unbeknownst to him, a tornado had formed above our alley, destroying everything in its path. Miraculously, our home remained intact.

The tornado's impact was felt throughout Lubbock, particularly in downtown and East Lubbock. My dad closed the restaurant early that night and offered shelter to two employees as power lines blocked their neighborhoods.

Sick Baby

When I was two years old, I spent around a month in the hospital, where I was diagnosed with three conditions: asthma, allergies, and epileptic seizures. Fortunately, I haven't had a seizure since then. I've been taking medication for it daily, and everything has been under control. However, there was a brief period when a doctor decided to adjust my medication to once a day instead of multiple times a day.

Unfortunately, this change triggered severe headaches. My mom wisely switched me back to the original schedule, and when we returned to the doctor, he agreed that she had made the right decision. He reinstated the original medication plan, and I've been doing well ever since.

I used to take my medication five times a day, but now it's been reduced to three times a day. However, I'm still taking the same medication I was prescribed as a child. When people asked me what I was taking or what it was for, I would often just say 'allergies' or 'allergies and asthma.' I found that if I mentioned 'epileptic seizures' or 'epilepsy,' people would treat me differently. They might exclude me from activities or be overly cautious around me, fearing something might happen. However, my condition is well-managed with the proper medication and a consistent schedule.

I realized that some kids and adults with similar conditions were treated differently, too. They might be left out or excluded due to fear or misunderstanding. That's why I preferred to downplay my condition and just mention 'allergies.' As a child, I didn't want to be treated differently or excluded by my peers or adults. I wanted to be seen as usual and included in activities without extra attention or concern. Because I had seen how others with similar conditions were treated differently, I appreciated my mom's efforts to give me a relatively everyday life. She encouraged me to participate in activities like playing, riding bikes, and skating.

I was also fortunate to have James, who taught me how to use a hammer at a young age, around five years old, when he was remodeling our kitchen. He shared many stories about his experiences, including some cautionary tales about skill saws, which I'm not too fond of!

Thanks to their support and guidance, I could lead a relatively normal childhood despite my condition. My mom's approach helped me feel included and allowed me to develop a sense of independence, which has been invaluable as I've grown older.

Tahoka Wedding Incident

In 1973, we attended a relative's wedding in Tahoka, where the bride had secretly spiked the punch. My mom, who rarely drank, unknowingly consumed some and was affected by the alcohol. After the wedding, she drove us back towards Lubbock but soon began to feel drowsy. She pulled over about 6 miles down the highway, where an older couple found us and checked on our well-being. They kindly let us use their phone, and my mom called my dad to come and pick us up. He arrived and took us safely home.

When my dad asked my mom what happened, she replied, "I don't know. I was fine, not tired at all, and suddenly I started feeling sleepy."

It wasn't until the next day that they discovered the truth - the punch at the wedding had been spiked with tasteless, odorless alcohol. Unbeknownst to my mom, she had consumed several cups of the punch, and some children even had some. The bride's decision to secretly add alcohol to the punch had put everyone at risk, and my mom was lucky to have been helped by the kind older couple.

Fairground Memories

A few years later, in either 1976 or 1977, my mom and I attended the fair, where we enjoyed our first concert featuring the Statler Brothers. We also explored the haunted house and possibly rode the Ferris wheel.

We returned to the fair around 1980, eager to revisit our favorite attractions. This time, we rode the Ferris wheel again, braved the haunted house, and tried the Hammerhead ride. Unbeknownst to us, the Hammerhead would stop at the top, upside down. My mom's wooden purse opened, scattering its contents – pills, billfold, and all – but fortunately, everything was recovered upon exiting the ride.

Memorable Trips

I have fond memories of going fishing with my grandmother. One particular story is from a trip my mom and I took to Arkansas in the late 1970s. My grandmother told us about when my uncle's grandfather's truck, with a camper attached, rolled back into the lake after slipping out of gear. The tow truck arrived, but the driver refused to enter the lake to hook up the cable. So, my uncle bravely swam down and attached the cable, allowing them to pull the entire truck out of the lake. The car was completely submerged underwater.

Visiting my grandmother in Arkansas and Oklahoma was always a treat. I fondly remember my uncle's pickup truck, which he had modified to sound like General Lee's horn from the Dukes of Hazzard. It was a fun touch that added to the excitement of our visits. I cherished the time spent with my cousins, grandmother, uncle, and aunt, creating memories that still make me smile. Those trips were a highlight of my childhood, filled with love, laughter, and adventure.

My grandmother joined my mom and me on several trips, creating lifelong memories. One highlight was our trip to Hawaii, where we enjoyed a nostalgic synchronized swimming show at a hotel reminiscent of the classic Esther Williams movies. Although they no longer offer this spectacle, I treasure the experience. We also explored Epcot, Walt Disney World, and other destinations. Our time together was always filled with laughter and joy, regardless of where we went. Those adventures with my grandmother and mom are cherished moments I'll always treasure.

Christmas at El Chico Restaurant

We'd set up Christmas trees at the El Chico restaurant every year. James had created a permanent base for the trees, gluing the trunks with epoxy. The trees stood about 10 feet tall and were stored in a nearby room during the off-season. To transport them, we'd wrap each tree tightly in a drop cloth, securing it in the back of the truck with anchors and ties in four directions. We'd drive carefully to storage, sealing any gaps in the drop cloth with tape. The trees would remain there until the following season. When it was time to decorate, we'd retrieve the trees from storage and transport them to one of two restaurants - El Chico, just three blocks away, or Otto's Granary, about five miles away. Driving down the street with a 10-foot tree standing upright in the back of the truck was always exciting. But we took pride in our secure transportation method, ensuring the trees arrived safely and traveled well.

My Love for Creating Miniature Furniture

I prefer using a jigsaw for cutting, but I'm also comfortable with a skilled saw. My mom and I enjoyed building projects using kits or scrap wood, like birdhouses and timers.

One of our favorite projects was a three-story tall, 6-foot long 'architectural house' - some might call it a dollhouse. We'd furnish and decorate each room with small light fixtures, furniture, and colors we liked, using it as a testing ground for our design ideas.

We'd even install tiny light fixtures and try out color schemes before applying them to our actual home. Like the Six Million Dollar Man, the house also served as a playground for my action figures. We'd create miniature furniture and accessories from scrap wood, fostering my creativity and love for building things.

Rubber Band Gun Story

Summer 1983 was a memorable time for us. Henry had been helping James remodel the Granary Restaurant while Armando enjoyed playing jokes on us. Armando tried to catch us off guard one hot summer day with water balloons, but I don't recall the specifics of his prank. What I do remember is the rubber band gun incident. Armando had been teasing us, and we decided to get our revenge. I crafted a rubber band gun, which we used to launch a surprise attack on Armando. It was a fun and playful way to retaliate against his constant joking.

Henry devised a clever idea - creating a rubber band gun to prank Armando. After work, he gathered scrap wood and crafted two guns, one handheld and one rifle-shaped, with grooves to hold multiple rubber bands. He added clothespins to secure the bands, allowing up to five shots simultaneously.

On Saturday morning, Henry picked me up early, and we grabbed donuts before heading to the restaurant. We waited in the kitchen for Armando, careful to avoid hitting him in the face. We ambushed him with a barrage of rubber bands when he arrived, catching him off guard. Armando laughed and conceded defeat, saying, "OK, y'all got me by surprise!"

After the prank, we sat down together, enjoying extra donuts and each other's company. It was a lighthearted moment filled with laughter and camaraderie. Our playful retaliation had brought us closer together, and we cherished the memory of that fun-filled morning.

Gene Wilder Chicago airport

In 1982, my mom and I were waiting to board our plane at Chicago airport, arriving early. We listened to the flight announcements and last calls. We noticed a services cart parked about waist-high and three feet wide in the middle of the busy walkway. Suddenly, a man in a full three-piece suit came sprinting towards us, shouting, "Hold the plane!" We thought he'd crash into the cart, but instead, he leaped over it, clearing the luggage without touching anything, and continued running.

He yelled, "Run to the gate!" as he disappeared into the crowd.

My mom and I were stunned, realizing we had just witnessed Gene Wilder, fresh from his iconic role as Willy Wonka and recent collaborations with Richard Pryor, making a desperate dash to catch his flight. We looked around, expecting cameras to capture the scene, but it was just a frantic passenger making his connection – which, impressively, he did!

Baseball Memory

When I was younger, my friends and I often played in the vacant lot across the street, hitting baseballs or playing frisbee golf. One afternoon, my dad came home from the restaurant and suggested we practice hitting baseballs together.

He grabbed his glove and said, "Come on, son, let's go!"

I always aimed to connect with the ball and hit it as far as possible. However, my swing didn't meet my ambitions on this particular day. The ball didn't go far at all; in fact, it hit my dad right below his belt. Let's just say it was a memorable moment!

After the incident with my dad, he decided to take a break from pitching to me. A few days later, James was working at our house and took a break to toss the ball for me to practice hitting. My dad warned him, "Watch out, James! That was no fluke what happened to me!" But James didn't listen. The first time I hit the ball, it struck him in the same spot as my dad - right below the belt. Both of them were in pain after getting hit with the baseball. Someone joked that I needed to stop aiming for them, but I protested, "I'm not aiming! I'm trying to hit the ball straight and as far as I can!"

That was the last time my Dad and James volunteered to pitch to me. You could say I made a lasting impression on them! From then on, they decided to leave the pitching to someone else. I couldn't blame them. After all, getting hit twice in the same spot was enough to make them retire from pitching duties for good!

Impressive Arrow Shot

My mom would often bring home large boxes of paper towels or toilet paper from the restaurant, which we'd store in the garage for household use. But we'd also repurpose some of these boxes for archery practice! We'd roll a box across the street, set a target sign on it, and take turns shooting arrows. One day, my first arrow missed the target by a hair's breadth, hitting the tree and bouncing off. But my next shot was a bullseye - literally! I hit the arrow lying on the ground, splitting it in half. It was a pretty impressive shot if I say so myself.

Learning to Ice Skate

My mom and I would often visit the market in Dallas, and in 1982, we discovered the joy of ice skating at the big mall in Dallas, which featured an ice-skating rink. To our surprise, learning to ice skate was much easier than learning to roller skate! After the initial fall, getting back up was a breeze, and ice skating became a delightful experience. We loved it so much that for three to four years, we'd make it a point to take a break from the market and spend afternoons ice skating. Initially, I was nervous, wondering how a single blade could support me, but it did! Given the choice, I'd always prefer ice skating over roller skating. There's something about gliding on ice that's just so much fun!

Ice Water Magic

In 1972, James, the restaurant manager, had a minor disagreement with my dad. Standing in the driveway, he came to our house and told my mom, "I can't work for your husband anymore!"

My mom was standing in the backyard near the garage door, holding a glass of ice water, when James tossed the keys at her feet. He was dressed in a suit. In response, she threw the glass of ice water on him and firmly told him she had no time for this, citing the sick baby inside who needed her attention. She instructed him to resolve the issue with Ken. James and my dad eventually settled their issue and continued working together for years.

To this day, James still tells how my mom 'cooled him off' with the glass of ice water. He jokes that on hot days, he remembers to beware of my mom's icy wrath, saying, 'Don't make her unhappy when she's got a glass of ice water in her hand - she might just use it to cool you off!'

Ted And Train

Between 1984 and 1986, I recall a lady named Rosa working as a cashier at the restaurant. Her husband, Ted, was an engineering major at Texas Tech, specializing in aerospace engineering. When I was around seven or eight, Ted created a model train board. The board measured approximately 3.5 to 4 feet wide and 6 feet long, with green grass-like material typically used for train layouts.

Later, when I was 14, Ted helped me build an even more giant model train board, measuring 3.5 to 4 feet wide and 7 feet long. We designed the layout and then went to Home Depot for materials. They cut the wood to our specifications. While loading the wood into our station wagon, one piece slipped from my hands and scratched the roof.

Although the damage was minor – I was upset by a quarter-inch by half-inch spot in the back. My mom was surprisingly calm, but I couldn't shake the feeling that I should have been more careful. Looking back, it was a valuable lesson: sometimes slowing down can prevent mistakes.

After bringing the boards home, Ted joined me the next day, a Saturday, to assemble the model train board. We secured the 2x4 frames around the wood's four sides using long screws, fastening them from the top down. Additional support came from two cross braces and six 4x4 legs, attached with large screws through the wood and into the legs. With two screws on each side reinforcing the 4x4 legs, the structure became sturdy.

Now, Ted and I can confidently stand on the train board without issues. Ted and I were setting up the train board, meticulously laying tracks, switches, and a turntable. However, Ted realized he'd left his soldering iron at Texas Tech's lab. Since it was Thanksgiving break, the campus was deserted, with only one police car in the parking lot. Undeterred, Ted drove his truck over parking bumpers and medians straight to the lab.

As we entered the lab, I reassured the officer, "It's fine, I know him."

Inside, Ted's workspace was cluttered. Drawers were open, with nuts, bolts, and screws spilled across the desk. He showed me his project, but I hesitated near the door, noticing a large radiation warning sign (about 3 feet wide and an inch thick).

Ted assured me, "Don't worry, Scott wouldn't bring anyone here. It's not safe, not even for my kids."

I watched in fascination as the laser beam bounced around the room. It hit the mirror, rebounded up to the ceiling, and traversed through troughs filled with various materials and thicknesses. The beam seamlessly navigated its path, reflecting off mirrors on the ceiling and passing through each of the four troughs.

I couldn't help but think, "Thank goodness everything is precisely aligned." Given the beam's potency, capable of burning through steel and lead, I worried about the potential consequences of a miscalculation. How quickly could it penetrate the drop ceiling and possibly damage the floor above? Fortunately, the team had a flawless safety record, avoiding such incidents.

This laser project was a side endeavor, complementing my primary work. I'd assist during summertime, Thanksgiving, Christmas breaks, and occasional weekends for about two years. I enjoyed these intermittent sessions, taking breaks from my routine to focus on the training project.

As time passed, our progress became tangible. We successfully set up the train track, constructed the train board, and built several accompanying structures. The project's gradual evolution was satisfying, and I looked forward to each work session.

We had made significant progress on the train project, with about half a dozen structures in place. Our next steps included building mountains and adding more details. However, life had other plans. My parents purchased a new house requiring extensive renovations, including new gas lines, plumbing, and electrical systems.

The remodeling process took eight long years, delaying our move-in date. During this time, we continued working on the train project in stages. We used mold ribbon to secure the turntable and disconnected the track where the two boards met. We ensured everything was nailed down, preparing for the eventual move.

When we finally relocated, we reassembled the boards in the attic room. Although the track is in place, I still need time to build the mountains and other landscape features. The buildings are stored, awaiting reassembly.

I remain committed to completing the project. It's just a matter of finding the time. Eventually, I'll uncover the buildings, set them up, and bring the training landscape to life.

Otto's Granary Adventures:

In 1984, Otto's Granary restaurant opened, and the manager who had launched the restaurant with my parents moved away. As a result, my mom took over as manager, bringing her experience from the previous restaurant. Interestingly, my mom and one of the other managers had visited a friend's barbecue restaurant, where they learned the art of adequately cutting barbecue and other tips from the trade. This experience would later benefit Otto's Granary, as they incorporated barbecue into their menu.

I fondly remember the four cooks at Otto's Granary restaurant, who were skilled in the kitchen and a joy to be around. They wore a distinctive uniform: a white shirt with a red scarf at the neck and a white chef's hat. This lively group of guys, including Mark, a former backup quarterback for the Texas Tech football team, and Mike, a wide receiver for the same team, brought a fun and lively atmosphere to the restaurant. Jeff's dad was a championship wrestler in Spain and Jeff would often share stories with us about him. They did an excellent job, and we were very proud of their work. This was around 1984-1985, but I think it might have been 1987—my memory isn't entirely clear on the exact date.

We had a talented chef called 'M' who from one of the local country clubs. He always worked on Sundays and brought a lot of enthusiasm to the kitchen. However, one Sunday, disaster struck when he used too much of a particular chemical to clean the grill, causing it to catch fire. The sprinkler system was activated, and the fire department arrived quickly. Fortunately, they extinguished the flames quickly.

But here's the thing: our 22 racks of ribs, freshly smoked and cooling, were covered in a fine powder from the sprinkler system. We were about to discard them, but the fireman surprisingly told us we could still use them. It was a close call, but everything turned out okay. We salvaged the ribs by putting them in pans and taking them with us despite the sprinkler powder on them. The firemen were understanding and even joked that they would 'eat well tonight!'

However, Chef M had another mishap while cleaning the fryers the following Sunday. He pulled one out too far, causing a gas leak behind it. When he tried to turn off the valve, it broke, and gas started leaking. He quickly grabbed a towel and held it around the leak to prevent a disaster, squatting down behind the fryer to contain the gas. This temporary fix allowed us to safely turn off the gas supply outside without hurting anyone. It was a close call, but we avoided another crisis thanks to Chef M's quick thinking!

James arrived just in time to cut off the gas supply, relieving Chef M, squatting behind the fryer for almost 45 minutes, holding a towel around the pipe to contain the leak. James replaced the valve and fixed the issue, returning everything to normal.

But, incredibly, the following Sunday, Chef M had another mishap while cleaning the large smoker in the kitchen. The smoker was an impressive piece of equipment, standing over 8 feet tall and 4 feet deep, with six sets of rotating shelves, each with two shelves. It was perfect for smoking ribs, brisket, and sausages. However, what happened this time? Did Chef M's cleaning efforts lead to another unexpected adventure?

When it was time to clean the smoker, Chef M volunteered. He'd done it before and was okay with getting inside the large smoker to scrub it thoroughly. He removed the shelves, the old charcoal and wood scraps from the firebox, and put them in a metal bucket. After finishing up, he stepped outside to stretch his legs and tossed the wood scraps into the dumpster, assuming they had cooled down. However, they were still hot, and when he returned inside, he carried the bucket containing the scraped-off grease and cleaning solution from the smoker. But here's what happened next...

Chef M overlooked the danger behind him as he returned to the restaurant. He had just emptied the grease and cleaning solution into the dumpster. Suddenly, the phone rang. The cashier from El Chico alerted us that the dumpster was on fire! We rushed to the back door and looked out to see Chef M walking towards us, oblivious to the flames erupting behind him. The dumpster was engulfed, and someone yelled that Chef M's clothes were on fire, too! It seemed he had been caught off guard, still carrying the bucket with remaining grease from the smoker, and hadn't noticed the fire spreading.

In a panic, Chef M grabbed the bucket and tossed its remaining contents into the dumpster, inadvertently fueling the fire. He then grabbed a small fire extinguisher, which did not match the growing flames. Fortunately, the fire department had already been called, and a firetruck arrived promptly. Two firefighters jumped out, grabbed a hose, and quickly sprayed the dumpster, extinguishing the fire. With a wave and a casual "see y'all," they drove off. Spaced just a month apart, those three Sundays were indeed eventful - it seemed like every Sunday brought a new adventure!

Later Adventures: Walt Disney World and Epcot

In 1985, we ventured to Walt Disney World and explored the wonders of Epcot. These experiences remain cherished memories, marking significant milestones in my life.

Memories of Epcot, Walt Disney World (1985)

My visit to Epcot at Walt Disney World in 1985 remains vivid. I recall exploring various educational rides, including one sponsored by Kodak. This ride showcased two distinct periods, from dinosaurs to the present day. Notably, it featured a restaurant in the middle, where vegetables were grown using innovative space-saving techniques.

The salads served were exceptional, among the best I've ever had. We also enjoyed other attractions, including a memorable encounter with C-3PO.

However, one ride stands out – a high-speed roller coaster disguised as a tram ride. Unbeknownst to my mom and me, it featured sudden acceleration, steep drops, and intense movements. We only discovered the warnings about heart conditions, seizures, and other health concerns after exiting the ride, relieved that we were both fine. Beyond the thrill rides, Walt Disney World offers an array of authentic restaurants. We dined at Italian, French, and German establishments, each featuring decorations and staff from its respective country.

A lighthearted moment occurred at the Italian or French restaurant when someone flirted with me, prompting my mom to tease, "One day, you'll find a wife here!" I playfully deflected, claiming I was too young and focused on our family store.

This experience showcases the magic of Walt Disney World, blending education, entertainment, and cultural immersion.

Nosy Neighborhood

My mom's station wagon was vital in our Halloween decorating adventure. We loaded cardboard coffins, pumpkins, and Jack-o-lanterns into the back and set off to decorate two restaurants. The coffins were a highlight, complete with old Halloween masks and clothes. After setting up the first display and receiving customer compliments, we returned home to load up the second coffin and decorations. Just then, a detective arrived at our door, responding to a concerned neighbor's calls about 'dead bodies' being carried out in coffins. The neighbor had watched too many crime shows! The detective, however, was understanding and even praised our display at El Chico, chuckling as he realized the 'bodies' were just props. With the matter cleared up, he went on his way, and we finished decorating the second restaurant's lobby for Halloween.

Pressing Party

One day, someone came to work and mentioned that their shirt wasn't pressed because they didn't know how to iron. This comment sparked an idea in my mom's mind. She remembered that Bobbie, the lady who usually did the ironing at our house, had been helping at the store, and I had to take time off to assist my parents out of town. So, my mom came up with the idea to host a 'pressing party' to help everyone learn how to iron and press their clothes.

There were likely over 50 shirts that needed pressing, and we managed to get through half or more of them. My mom made it a fun event by ordering pizza and having root beer arrive later. She set up four ironing boards with irons and enlisted my help, along with my best friend and one or two employees who wanted to join. It turned into a productive and enjoyable 'pressing party.'

Five people, plus my mom and me, participated in the pressing party. She started by teaching us when to do the yokes and when to do the sleeves, and then we rotated down the line, eventually learning how to press an entire shirt. Word got around because the next day, one or two employees approached us and asked when we would have the next pressing party and if they could join in and learn how to iron a shirt.

The pressing party was an effective way to learn this valuable skill, and others appreciated it. We accomplished tasks that needed attention while having a productive and social experience. As a result, everyone had nicely neat, pressed shirts for the future, and they no longer had to rely on their parents to iron them. Wearing a nicely pressed or ironed shirt to work is essential, especially when we wear specific ties. Still, even without ties, it's crucial to present oneself professionally and look one's best.

A Birthday Tradition Born at My Parents' Restaurant:

In the late 80s or early 90s, my parents' restaurant servers created an infectious birthday song, sparking a beloved tradition. Patrons began requesting the special song, and two unique versions emerged. Here's one:

Birthday Song Number 1: Revised

(All servers clapping)

All: Here we come, just a walkin' down the street,

Singing happy, happy, happy birthday to you.

We have a sopapilla 'cuz the apple pie ain't free,

Singing happy, happy, happy birthday to you.

Leader: You look good!

All: You look good!

Leader: You look fine!

All: You look fine!

ALL: You look good - You look fine.

You should eat here all the time,

Singing happy, happy, happy birthday to you!

The servers' energetic performance added to the song's charm. A lead server would start singing 30-50 feet from the table, accompanied by two servers behind and two more behind them. Other staff members would join in, forming a procession of 7-9 singers, clapping and spreading out to either side as they approached the birthday person. This joyful spectacle became a signature experience at my parents' restaurant, making birthdays unforgettable for countless patrons.

A Golfing Tradition Cut Short by Fate:

In their youthful days, Scott and David shared a passion for golf, forging a bond that transcended time and distance. As high school friends, they would often tee off together. Even as their paths diverged in college – Scott attending Texas Tech and David enrolling at Texas A&M – their love for golf remained constant.

When they reunited in Lubbock in the mid-1990s, they decided to revive their golfing tradition. David took a break from his thriving business, and Scott stepped away from his responsibilities. Their plan was to meet weekly and relive old times.

The first outing was a success. They played the front nine, savored lunch together, and conquered the back nine. As they scheduled their next tee time, enthusiasm filled the air.

But fate had other plans. The night before their second outing, the skies darkened, and torrential rains poured. The deluge continued through the night, leaving the golf course inundated. The following day, Scott and David arrived to find the course closed, its lush greens submerged underwater. Only half of the flag on the green remained visible, a poignant symbol of their dashed hopes.

The course remained closed for an entire year, undergoing extensive repairs. Scott and David's weekly golfing ritual was put on hold.

Undeterred, they reconnected once the course reopened. Eager to rekindle their tradition, they scheduled another tee time. But history repeated itself. Within 24 hours of their second tee time, the heavens opened up again, and the course was again flooded, forcing another year-long closure.

Scott and David's determination never wavered. They remained committed to their golfing camaraderie, awaiting the course's reopening and the chance to tee off again. Scott and David returned to the golf course, determined to play uninterrupted. They finished their round, scheduled their next tee time, and awaited the following week.

But, as if on cue, the course flooded for the third time within 24 hours of their next game. Although better drainage had been installed, the entire course was underwater. This time, recovery was faster. Within six months, part of the back nine reopened, while the front nine remained submerged. It took over a year for the course to fully recover.

As fate would have it, Scott's avid golfer father began planning the annual Father's Day tournament. While overseeing concrete work at his house, he turned to Scott and David with excitement and trepidation, "This will be my first Father's Day tournament in over three years. Every year, the course floods, and I miss it."

Scott and David exchanged knowing glances, prompting Scott's father to warn sternly, "Don't you two dare step on that course until after the tournament! I don't want it to flood again and ruin another Father's Day."

Scott and David couldn't help but chuckle at the superstition surrounding their golf outings. Would their next game break the flooded course curse? I've cherished golfing at the course since I was around eight years old, sharing laughter and camaraderie with my friends Ronnie and, later, David. Our group's dynamics were built on respect and sportsmanship. We drove the golf cart responsibly, staying on designated paths to preserve the lush greens.

Under James the Carpenter's guidance, I honed my golfing skills. He not only taught me the game but also gifted me my first bowling ball for my birthday and taught me how to bowl. James' patience and expertise helped me become a decent golfer.

Though we didn't golf as frequently as we'd like, our outings were always special. Little did I know our recent flooding incidents had sparked a humorous conspiracy theory. The man pouring the sidewalk, eager for the Father's Day golf tournament, surprisingly blamed David and me for the course's repeated flooding. It seemed our coincidental tee times had become a running joke, with some believing we were the "flood catalysts."

Ronnie and David exchanged amused glances, and I couldn't help but chuckle at the absurdity. Who would have thought our love for golf would be linked to the whims of the weather?

Golfing Adventures: Wind, Water, and Wayward Clubs

Another golf outing with Tommy proved memorable as gusty winds swept across the course. With 30-mile-per-hour gusts, Tommy turned to me and said, "What do you think, sir? Shall we tackle the first nine right into the wind?"

I nodded, embracing the challenge. "It's not stormy, just windy. We'll do well into the wind and think of how good we'll do on a calm day!"

We rose to the occasion, staying in the middle of the fairway, avoiding houses lining the holes. Mother Nature's obstacles only added to the excitement. However, a later outing with James, David, and a few friends took an unexpected turn. One of our companions hit his ball into the lake. Instead of taking a penalty stroke, he reacted impulsively.

In a moment of frustration, he hurled his driver into the lake, watching in awe as it spun through the air like a helicopter blade. Reality soon set in.

"Wait, I need that club!" he exclaimed, wading into the water to retrieve his submerged driver. We burst into laughter at the absurdity.

James chuckled, "Well, that's one way to test your club's buoyancy!" David quipped, "Guess that's what they mean by 'taking a plunge' in golf!"

Our group's camaraderie and banter turned an embarrassing moment into an unforgettable story.

As our friend's driver splashed into the lake, the rest of us waited patiently, our golf balls already on the green or fairway. But he was determined to retrieve his club. Ignoring the rule against entering the water, he asked for help. I handed him my 12-foot ball retriever, and our group formed a human chain: one guy held his hand, David grasped the next, then me, and finally, James, ensuring our friend's stability.

He stretched, straining to reach the club, but fell short by inches. The water's edge was his limit; he wouldn't venture further, fearing the unknown depths. With a sigh, he declared, "Never mind, I'll leave it." Then, with a mischievous grin, he added, "I'll come back tonight and get it." We exchanged skeptical glances, wondering if he was serious. The incident became a running joke for the rest of the day. Our friend chuckled about his failed rescue attempt, and we playfully teased him.

As we continued our game, the lake's secrets remained intact, including whether or not he returned for his submerged driver. The mystery remained unspoken, but the memory of his antics lingered, entertaining us throughout our round.

Different Flavors of Drinks

I remember we acquired two new machines for making cappuccinos and lattes, and we were excited to experiment with various flavors. We had at least 8-10 different syrup flavors to try, and we combined some and used others on their own. To help you visualize the setup, imagine walking into the store and heading 12 feet to the right. Then, go about 25 feet back, passing through two doorways, and you'll find yourself in the back room where the two machines are located. This is where we perfected our craft, trying different flavor combinations and techniques to create the perfect drinks.

Julie walked into the store and approached Scott, who was training Tiffany. "Scott, would you like to have a drink?" Scott nodded in agreement. She then headed to the back room, hidden from view by a wall that nearly reached the ceiling, making it impossible for her to hear the conversation at the register.

Tiffany turned to me and whispered, "You have no idea what kind of drink you'll get."

I confidently replied, "It'll be a crème brûlée cappuccino in a few minutes."

Right on cue, Julie reappeared around the corner, carrying two drinks - one for me and one for herself. "Let me know what you think about the crème brûlée cappuccino," she said, prompting Tiffany's bewildered expression.

The next day, during Tiffany's register training, Julie would often experiment with unique flavors. One day, Julie told Scott, "I'm thinking of making a drink." Scott agreed, and Julie disappeared into the back room, out of sight.

Tiffany turned to me and whispered, "You're getting a crème brûlée cappuccino."

But I disagreed, "No, I think it'll be a coconut latte."

Tiffany insisted, "Yesterday was crème brûlée. Today will be the same." I chuckled, knowing Julie and I hadn't discussed flavors.

Just then, Julie reappeared with two drinks. "Let me get your thoughts on the coconut cappuccino," she said, surprising Tiffany.

Julie walked in on the third day of Tiffany's training and said, "I'm thinking of making one drink." Scott agreed, and Julie headed to the back room. I predicted, "It'll be an Italian cream soda with raspberry." Tiffany was skeptical, given our focus on hot drinks. But when Julie returned with the drink, I was correct—an Italian cream soda with raspberry.

Julie and I shared an unspoken understanding as if we were connected through our love of creative flavors.

Julie and I shared an uncanny understanding honed from over a year of working together. We could anticipate each other's thoughts, even without explicitly discussing flavors. Tiffany, still in training, was understandably perplexed by our silent communication. The COVID-19 pandemic brought unprecedented challenges, but Otto's Granary was fortunate. As purveyors of coffee, tea, chocolate, and gourmet foods, we were deemed essential. This allowed us to continue operating and adapt to curbside service for our customers.

Interestingly, the pandemic also sparked a surge in puzzle sales. During uncertain times, people sought comfort in comforting treats and activities. We were grateful to provide both, ensuring our customers' well-being while keeping our business thriving.

Strange Coincidences

I recall the year 2000 vividly, an election year that brought more than just political change. It was a year of unusual weather patterns, with snowfall on every major holiday—Thanksgiving, Christmas, New Year's, Valentine's Day, St. Patrick's Day, and Easter. The relentless snow became a hallmark of that year. Amidst the winter wonderland, my mom embarked on a trip to Dallas, a journey that stands out in my memory alongside the snowy milestones.

My mom had undergone knee replacement surgery and needed to visit her doctor in Dallas for a check-up. It was snowy, and Heidi mentioned that her car couldn't handle the conditions. She had a friend who could drop her off but needed a ride home. I offered to help, saying, "I'll drop you off after work." We made plans for me to pick her up and drive her home from the store. After work, I dropped her off at her apartment complex, waiting until she safely entered the building before heading home.

Then, I went upstairs to talk to my dad and have some tea. Earlier, the guys at the store had been discussing a movie, possibly Lord of the Rings, and one had even dressed up to see it in the theater. I turned on the T.V. that Friday night and stumbled upon the movie. I wanted to watch a bit, but it reminded me of Alice in Wonderland, with the characters seeming more prominent than the houses. The next thing I knew, I was waking up to the credits rolling. I flipped the channel to Westerns or American Movie Classics and caught an old Cary Grant film before dozing off again.

The next day at work, a coworker asked me if I had watched Lord of the Rings. I mentioned I'd seen it the night before but found it okay, comparing it to Alice in Wonderland and admitting I fell asleep before the good part. Just then, Heidi walked in, looked at me, and said nothing as if she knew something I didn't. The co-worker looked at me and said, "Don't say anything," then he turned to Heidi and said, 'What did you think of Lord of the Rings? I know you've seen it.'

Heidi replied, "Funny, you ask. I saw it last night. The wagon scene reminded me of Alice in Wonderland, with the strange proportions of the people and houses."

Our co-worker seemed puzzled, saying, 'You saw it with Scott, right?'

I clarified, 'No, I was at home.' My co-worker appeared skeptical as if he thought we were together watching the movie. The co-worker never believed that Heidi and I watched the same movie at the same time and did not even talk about watching it beforehand. He also said we watched it together; however, I watched it at home, and Heidi was in her apartment.

For the rest of the year, this became a recurring joke. He would ask what Heidi and I watched and vice versa; he would never believe the coincidence.

My mom and I would watch a different Christmas movie every second or third night of November and December, like Home Alone, a Cary Grant film, or a John Wayne western, and when asked, we'd share what we saw. But our coworker never believed us, convinced we were secretly watching Lord of the Rings together. It was a strange coincidence that we'd all seen the movie simultaneously.

Hectic Relocation

In the spring and summer of 2004, we began working on the Granary, preparing it for the transition. We planned to get everything ready, including setting up shelves, moving merchandise, and even preparing Christmas displays in advance. However, things don't always go as planned. Meanwhile, we had recently moved into an older house that my parents and I had spent about 8-10 years remodeling. Unexpectedly, my dad's friend approached him with an offer: someone was willing to pay cash for our old house immediately. While this was a great opportunity, we had intended to hold onto the house for a bit longer, utilizing one of the workrooms and the office building on the back of the property.

In the early spring of 2005, we moved both the house and the store. The house sold, and we had a two-week window to vacate the premises. After 35 years, we had accumulated significant belongings, so we rented a couple of storage units just two blocks from the store and our old house. This way, we could temporarily store some household items, transport them to the new house, sort through them, and either unpack, sell, or give away what we no longer needed. It was a busy time, juggling the store and house move simultaneously.

After completing the house move, we refocused on the store, temporarily storing some items in a nearby storage unit to free up space for unpacking and organization. The storage unit already held seasonal items, old restaurant equipment, and other goods.

However, during lunch one day, the storage unit owner informed us that the property had sold but assured us we'd receive a six-month notice before any changes. Just two weeks later, he returned with an apology, revealing that we now had only two weeks to vacate the storage unit. This meant we had to move the store's contents again, finding new storage units farther away—about 3-4 miles—and transferring the essential items from one storage facility to another. That summer was indeed a challenging one. We had to move my family's 35-year-old home, the 20-year-old store, and contents from multiple storage units. To manage the workload, we worked on storage during the day and the store at night, as it was easier to focus without daytime disruptions. Although it took us a month longer than expected to complete the move, the mall graciously allowed us to stay an extra month, which was a huge relief. The new storage facility manager was accommodating, providing us with a unique access code to work beyond the usual 8 p.m. curfew. We often found ourselves loading or unloading trucks at the mall or storage units until 2 a.m. By summer's end, we had rented around eight storage units, ranging from 10x20 to smaller 6x6 units, and eventually returned the smaller ones once we'd unpacked. It was a hectic and eventful summer, but we persevered and got everything moved and organized.

Remodeling Our Dream Home

When we purchased an older house, we embarked on a remodeling journey. As we began stripping the walls of outdated wallpaper, we uncovered a surprise: nine layers of paper. But that was just the beginning.

In the bathroom, a vibration caught our attention. Our skilled carpenter, James, investigated and discovered worn copper wiring from the 1920s or 1930s. We realized the house needed extensive upgrades in electrical, plumbing, and gas lines. Demolishing the downstairs bathroom revealed a hidden gem. We found the inscription on the back of a large mirror: '1934, Fort Smith, Arkansas.' Interestingly, that was my grandmother's hometown. We took our time remodeling, staying in our other house until the project's completion. Our team consisted of James, my mom, and me, with occasional help from my dad, friends, and other carpenters. We made many memories, working together and overcoming challenges.

However, unexpected issues arose. A snowstorm caused one of the roofs to collapse, prompting James to brace it temporarily. We enlisted Nolan's expertise and an engineer's assessment, leading to necessary roofing structure updates.

The original garage-turned-bedroom attic had 2x4 ceiling joists instead of 2x12s. We corrected this and began constructing a new roof. But fate intervened: the day we started cutting into the roof, a torrential rainstorm hit. Despite our efforts to cover the exposed area, water seeped in.

The aftermath required tearing out and redoing the kitchen cabinets, floor, and adjacent laundry room's sheet rock. Although the process took longer, we persevered and completed the remodel.

Our journey taught us patience, teamwork, and creative problem-solving. The result was worth the effort: a beautifully restored home filled with memories.

Memories of Our Home Renovation Journey

I'm grateful for James, our trusted carpenter, who ensured my safety during the renovation. He intervened when I was working tirelessly, preventing potential heat stroke. A passerby later confirmed James' concern. James, a skilled carpenter and mentor, has worked with us for years. His expertise proved invaluable, mainly when unexpected issues arose.

Our area experienced record-breaking rainfall during the renovation, causing the Lakeridge golf course to flood. Our house suffered damage, requiring extensive repairs.

One day, James suffered an accident while drilling. His hammer drill hit a nail, causing the handle to flip back and break his wrist. Despite his stubbornness, James continued to advice and work with a cast.

My friend David and I shared laughter-filled moments with James. We cut down a dead tree, taking necessary safety precautions. James entertained us with Aggie jokes during our break until David retaliated with a clever punchline, leaving James momentarily speechless.

Later, water seepage in the basement required attention. Specialists dug a large hole to locate the leak, eventually finding a rock-punctured hole in the waterproof membrane.

They repaired and reinforced the area, ensuring no further leaks.

Our journey taught us resilience, teamwork, and problem-solving. We cherished moments of camaraderie and learned from unexpected challenges.

Mistaken Call from the Hospital

Around 2013, about three years before she passed away, my mom received a devastating phone call from her doctor's office on a Friday night. They informed her that her test results showed she had kidney cancer. I remember going to her room and discussing the news with her, as our bedrooms are all upstairs, while my dad's room is downstairs. We decided not to tell him about it over the weekend, as he was already concerned about his age and potential health risks, such as falling on the stairs. Instead, we focused on figuring out a plan and arranging things for the future without unnecessarily worrying him. However, on Monday afternoon, the doctor's office called back with an astonishing correction: they had made a mistake, giving her someone else's test results. Thankfully, my mom was okay, and we were all relieved.

One reason we didn't tell my dad about my mom's initial cancer diagnosis was that he had just had heart surgery the year before.

I recall a poignant encounter some years later while walking across the parking lot between my store and my parents' restaurant. A man, who regularly parked between the two businesses, stopped me and expressed his condolences, saying my parents were missed and that I was doing an excellent job with the restaurant and store. I thanked him, and he shared that he had recently received devastating news from his doctor - he had only a few months to live due to cancer. I tried to offer some encouragement, pointing out that he was still mobile, not in significant pain, and could enjoy some activities, like getting out and about. He initially thought I couldn't find a bright side, but I countered that his ability to move around and enjoy small pleasures was a positive aspect. He agreed, acknowledging that I had found a bright side for him.

A Memorable Trip to the Cotton Bowl

In the late stages of Spike Dykes' tenure at Texas Tech, my friends and I embarked on an unforgettable adventure to the Cotton Bowl. Texas Tech faced off against USC in what was our first bowl game experience.

While booking our accommodations in Dallas, I encountered confusion. The hotel claimed no knowledge of the Red Raider Club's reserved rooms. Only when I mentioned USC did they locate the listing.

Upon arrival, we dined at the newly opened Planet Hollywood. The atmosphere buzzed with Texas Tech and USC fans. Raider Red, Texas Tech's mascot, appeared, sparking a spirited sing-off between fans of both teams.

After dinner, David suggested visiting Hooters Restaurant and Bar. As we trailed behind him, the establishment suddenly closed, disappointing David.

The next day, we attended the football game, filled with excitement despite Texas Tech's loss. A notable incident occurred when USC fans removed Raider Red's mustache, prompting a temporary exit for repairs. The crowd's chants brought him back for the fourth quarter. Following the game, we headed to the airport, where a plane awaited Red Raider Club members. We enjoyed a meal onboard, reflecting on our exhilarating experience.

Hawaii 2012

I cherish the memories of our family trip to Hawaii with my Great Aunt Joy. It was her first time visiting the islands, while my mom and I had been fortunate enough to visit a few times before, including trips with my grandmother.

We departed Lubbock at 09:00 a.m. and arrived in Oahu around 02:00 p.m., with a brief 20-minute layover in Dallas. We felt lucky to have made our connection. After landing, we headed to our Waikiki hotel, checked in, and enjoyed a delicious meal at the hotel's outdoor restaurant.

Following lunch, we freshened up in our room and then set out to explore. We took a taxi to the mall, where my mom needed to replace her shoes after an unexpected mishap. The rest of the day was spent soaking up the island atmosphere.

The next day, Saturday, my mom and I had scheduled doctor's appointments. We visited a kind and caring doctor in a five-story building conveniently located near a charming toy store. Outside the store, a person dressed in a bear costume greeted passersby, adding to the warm and welcoming atmosphere. After visiting the doctor's office, where my mom received treatment for her foot or sore throat and I was diagnosed with swimmer's ear, we spent the day exploring and enjoying ourselves. We had dinner at the hotel that night. The next day, we attended a traditional Hawaiian luau. After returning, we strolled around Waikiki, browsing shops and discovering an art gallery that caught my attention around midnight.

Back in our hotel room around 01:00 a.m., my mom and Aunt Joy's laughter filled the air. Suddenly, a knock at the door interrupted our joyful moment. I peeked through the peephole and saw hotel security and a police officer. I opened the door slightly, and they asked, "Is everything okay, sir?" They explained that there had been noise complaints and needed to verify my mom's well-being. I invited them in, and they greeted my mom and Aunt Joy.

After a brief check, they asked me to keep the noise down. Then, surprisingly, they requested my driver's license for verification. They snapped a photo of it and left. Chuckling, I teased my mom and Aunt Joy, "You two are trying to get me in trouble!" They laughed, and we continued our evening.

As we lunched at Neiman Marcus, Aunt Joy noticed my repeated refills of iced tea and teased, "You're really enjoying that drink!" I chuckled, knowing I had opted for a non-alcoholic choice due to my epilepsy medication.

Aunt Joy jokingly warned, "You won't be able to walk after all those refills!"

I confidently replied, "I'll be fine."

After visiting the restroom, Aunt Joy exclaimed, "You're handling it remarkably well! How are you still walking?" I smiled, revealing the secret, "It's just pineapple juice and iced tea!"

Aunt Joy playfully accused, "You have alcohol in that drink!"

I clarified, "No, ma'am, I'm having iced tea and pineapple juice."

She laughed, confusing it with Long Island iced tea.

My mom and Aunt Joy enjoyed a glass of wine with lunch, their favorite – a pink champagne cocktail with raspberry at the Mariposa.

That afternoon, we explored Oahu's sights. We embarked on a delightful dinner cruise and savored dinner at the Royal Hawaiian.

During dinner at the Royal Hawaiian, my mom's fried fish dish arrived with a startling presentation – the whole fish facing her! She playfully turned the plate to face Aunt Joy, then me, sparking laughter from the servers.

Our daily routine consisted of breakfast at 07:30 a.m., departing the hotel by 08:30 a.m., and returning briefly to freshen up or change. We packed our schedule with activities, exploring Oahu from 09:00 a.m. to 06:00 a.m.

My mom arranged a car service through the hotel concierge, costing between $80 and $100. The first day brought a limo, while subsequent days brought a town car.

Other activities included:

- Dinner Cruise

- Exploring Waikiki

- Neiman Marcus lunch

- Royal Hawaiian dinner

After visiting the tea supplier, we headed to Pearl Harbor but decided to observe from a distance due to the long lines.

Instead, we asked our driver for lunch suggestions and visited the Dole Plantation. We savored mustard and chili dogs with pineapple, a signature ingredient in many of their menu items.

Next, we explored the Polynesian Cultural Center, where we stumbled upon a tram tour reminiscent of those at Universal Studios.

Our driver took us on a surprise detour through the neighborhood, passing the Mormon Temple. We enjoyed the scenic route, watching an informative movie during the 15-20 minute wait before returning.

My mom, Aunt Joy, and I were the only passengers on this tranquil tour, making it a unique and relaxing experience.

After visiting the Polynesian Cultural Center, we reflected on the historical film's accuracy, comparing it to the 1966 movie "Hawaii" starring Julie Andrews and Richard Harris. We explored the center's grounds, vowing to spend a full day there on our next visit. The 2012 center had expanded significantly since our 1979 visit.

Next, we freshened up for the delightful dinner cruise. The following day, our car service took us to the North Shore, where we visited a soap company whose products we sold at Greenery.

Our driver, a Texan-turned-Hawaiian resident, shared hidden gems and filming locations. She pointed out the palace used as the Five-0 headquarters in Hawaii Five-0 and mentioned that the exterior had been damaged in the previous season's finale and was undergoing repairs.

She also showed us areas where movies were filmed, giving us a unique perspective on the island. Passing the BYU campus and enjoying the scenic North Shore added to the day's pleasure.

Our six-day Oahu adventure culminated with a thrilling helicopter tour. Then, we headed to Maui for a three-day getaway.

However, our first day on Maui was marred by my unexpected illness - a headache and nausea. My mom and

Aunt Joy graciously opted to stay with me at the hotel, forgoing exploration.

Feeling guilty for holding them back, I spent the afternoon recovering. Later, we enjoyed dinner at the hotel restaurant, entertained by hula dancers and live music.

Fortunately, I woke up the next day feeling much better. Our concierge arranged a private tour with an affable older driver, who chauffeured us in his Lincoln Town Car.

We visited a unique winery that produces pineapple wine, along with other fruit-infused varieties like passionfruit. Our driver recommended Mama's Restaurant for lunch, a hidden gem away from tourist crowds.

Our driver recommended Mama's Restaurant, a hidden gem unknown to many tourists. He praised the eatery's unique approach, with daily menus dictated by the freshest catches from local fishermen.

We savored a delicious meal and then visited a quaint, old saloon-style building. Our driver revealed that this was Kris Kristofferson's favorite haunt, and Willie Nelson would occasionally drop by for impromptu jam sessions.

"Sometimes it's one of them, sometimes both," he said. "They might bring friends or fellow musicians for an informal performance." He emphasized that these sessions were unannounced, making every visit a delightful surprise.

Before taking us to this spot, our driver hesitated, worried it might be too rough around the edges. However, he assured us it was worth visiting despite its rustic charm.

We continued our tour, exploring Maui's picturesque landscapes and snapping photos along the way. At one stop, the wind was so strong that it blew the car door back, leaving us laughing.

After snapping photos, our driver mentioned the strong wind had dented the car door. "No worries, I shouldn't have parked here," he chuckled, attributing it to the gusty conditions.

We continued exploring Maui, visiting a prestigious golf club frequented by PGA players. Although none were present that day, we saw photos of over a dozen renowned golfers on the walls. A tournament was scheduled to take place just days after our departure.

Our driver showed us a historic hotel featured in an old Cary Grant film. Later, we strolled through Lahaina, browsing gift shops, admiring docked boats, and enjoying lunch at an Italian restaurant with a charming deck.

A highlight was visiting Banyan Tree Park, home to the largest Banyan tree in Maui. We also discovered an art gallery and other hidden gems.

Although some of these places were lost in a fire a few years later, we cherished the memories of our time on the island.

My Maui adventure with my mom and Aunt Joy remains unforgettable, but unfortunately, we never got to return together, as they have since passed away. However, I hold onto the hope of revisiting Hawaii one day.

During our 1979 trip, we stumbled upon a film set while walking. My mom inquired and learned that the cast of Gilligan's Island had just finished filming. We missed meeting the stars by mere minutes.

That evening, we dined at a restaurant featuring Don Ho's live performance. He famously invited a child on stage during each show, and my mom was asked if I'd like to participate. However, I was shy, tired, and struggling to stay awake after a busy day.

Despite that missed opportunity, we cherished every moment in Hawaii. The warm hospitality and friendly locals made our trips truly special.

Hawaii's beauty and charm have stayed with me, and I look forward to returning someday.

Close-Knit Family

At a recent wedding, I caught up with some cousins from my mom's side. I have a few cousins on my dad's side but many more on my mom's. I told them, "You know, quite a few of us!"

One cousin replied, "There are a lot of us!"

I nodded in agreement and said, "You can say we're a large family with small family values." Even though some of us hadn't seen each other in seven years, it felt like no time had passed.

My cousin smiled and said, "Exactly! It's like no time is lost." We both acknowledged that despite our large numbers, our family values remain solid and close-knit.

I coined the phrase 'large family with small family values' because many people assume that with a big family comes disconnection. But that's not true for us. Despite our numbers, we're close-knit, and everyone gets along. I'm grateful to have such a wonderful family. My cousins and I discussed how some of us are right in the middle—not the youngest, not the oldest—and how that's created a special bond. We've got younger cousins who still have fun with the older ones, and vice versa. Age doesn't matter; everyone's always a joy to be around. Being in the middle means connecting with both the teens and the sixty-somethings, and it's fantastic to see how well everyone clicks.

Early 1960s

The Clown was inspired by Bozo the Clown. I was six years old when I painted it.

The other two paintings were inspired by the El Chico menu cover early, sometime between 1985 and 1993.

This picture is from 1981—Otto's Granary Kiosk at South Plains Mall.

I did this painting in 1983 when I was 13 years old.

These are the two paintings we did in the summer of 1980 at the little art class in which my mom enrolled me, herself, and my best friend, Ronnie.

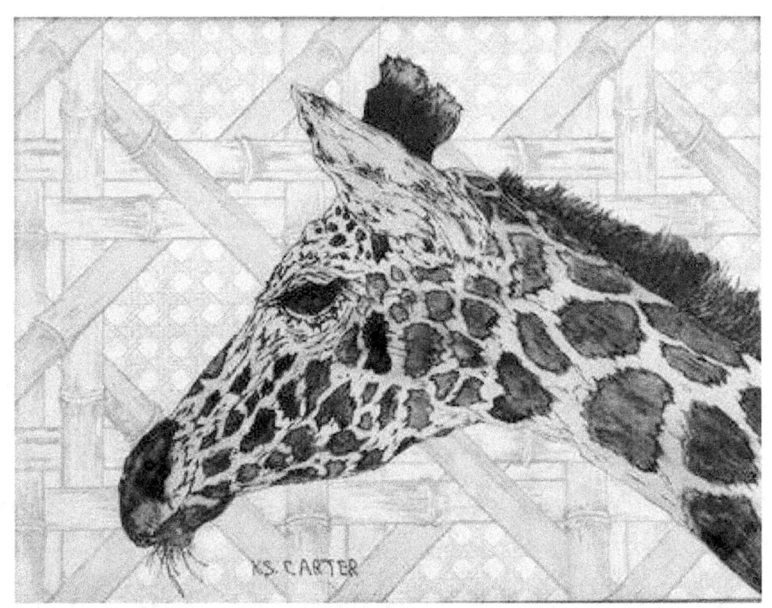

These are some of my paintings from when Mrs. Thornton taught me about painting and drawing on glass.

In Otto's building, around 1980, James looks like he's on a pile of woodworking on the display window of the attic store.

My parents' restaurant operated from September 1969 to December 2019.

My parents' 2nd restaurant operated from June 1979 to June 1999.

Otto's building around 2020 & 2018

Christmas 2018